A CIVILIAN COUNSELOR'S PRIMER FOR COUNSELING VETERANS

2nd Edition

Herbert A. Exum, Ph.D.
Jose E. Coll, Ph.D.
Eugenia L. Weiss, Psy.D.

Linus
Publications, Inc.

Published by Linus Publications, Inc.
Deer Park, NY 11729

ISBN: 1-60797-175-5

Printed in the United States of America.

Print Number 5   4   3   2   1

Table of Contents

CHAPTER 03

Counseling and Services in the Military

CHAPTER 04

The Impact of Combat on Veterans & Counselors Interacting with Military Personnel

CHAPTER 05

CHAPTER 06

CHAPTER 07

CHAPTER 08

Appendix A

Appendix B

Appendix C

Appendix D

Appendix E

Appendix F

References

Acknowledgement

We would like to dedicate this book to all of the men and women who have served in the United States Armed Forces and who continue to serve our nation against foreign and domestic enemies.

Our most sincere appreciation goes to Allison Santoyo who dedicated countless hours during the summer of 2010 to ensure mission accomplishment.

To our families who have accompanied us through the unforgiving seas of writing and professional accomplishments, without their support we would not be where we are today.

Preface

Why we need a primer to counsel veterans and their families

Since the end of the draft, the majority of civilian counselors and therapists have in all probability had little consistent exposure to individuals who have served in the armed forces and may know very little about military culture or the problems and issues faced by enlisted military personnel, veterans and their families. Most of what civilians, including mental health professionals, know about service members is typically what they may have witnessed on television or in the movies. The actual lives of service members and their families tend to be much more complex than what they are depicted as in the mass media.

Military personnel form a distinct sub-set, or sub-culture of American society and as such, are governed by a separate set of laws, norms, traditions and values than the civilian population. Thus, individuals who leave the military after many years of active duty service experience the same type of culture shock as any other newcomer to the American culture. These individuals share the same sense of disorientation, change of status and loss of identity as immigrants adjusting to a host culture. In veterans, there is a search for a new identity and an effort to recreate meaning, and often they are met with unfavorable societal attitudes or conditions.

Some military personnel who return to civilian life after service in the military will face serious adjustment issues. Some will return having lost trust in the U.S. government and in American foreign policy; others will doubt their religious beliefs and faith. Many military personnel will return to civilian life with physical disabilities caused by accidents, combat injuries, or sometimes-unknown environmental factors both within and external to the war zone. Still another group will return with less apparent disabilities, psychological and emotional injuries resulting from combat experiences, witnessing the death of civilians (non-combatants), or by being victims of sexual assault, often perpetrated by peers.

Civilian counselors and other health care professionals need to identify the signs of distress among military personnel, veterans, and their families, while establishing and maintaining a therapeutic alliance.

In order to promote the development of this alliance, and ultimately be successful in their treatment efforts, it is important for civilian mental health professionals to have a fundamental understanding of American military history, the role of military culture, and the mission of the military when working with service members and their families.

Overview

This primer is based on the notion that the training, socialization and indoctrination into the U.S. armed forces creates belief systems, values and a lifestyle among service members (and their dependents) that is different than those of the civilian world. These differences warrant the utilization of the term "military culture," as we address the needs of this segment of the U.S. population.

Having military experience alters service members on several levels. There are physical transformations that military training produces in service members as well as behavioral changes. However, few are cognizant of the significant impact that military socialization has on the way service members interact with one another and with the civilian population, especially once service members part from the military. Most veterans seem to be able to readjust to a civilian lifestyle with relatively little difficulty. This group of veterans is apparently able to integrate the values, traditions and behaviors of military culture with those of civilian culture and lead satisfying lives outside of the military. However, for a variety of reasons, other veterans are not able to make the transition back to civilian society as easily. This primer will address the issues, challenges and needs of this segment of the U.S. veteran population.

The primer is designed primarily for civilian counselors and other human services professionals who encounter this vulnerable group of veterans and/or their families. These helping encounters take place in a multitude of settings. For example, veterans are seen at Veterans Administration Medical Centers, Vet Centers, university and community college counseling centers, community mental health centers, private offices, and in other human services agencies and facilities. The purpose of this primer is to provide professionals (as well as student interns) who serve these clients, the fundamental information they need to work successfully with this population. The reader will learn about military training and culture, the types of stressors service members' confront, the psychological disorders they are likely to present with, the impact of these disorders and stressors on the family and the various treatment options currently available.

A significant portion of this primer is devoted to discussing the historical, philosophical, and sociopolitical perspectives of the American armed forces. An exploration of this broader perspective provides practitioners a context for understanding military culture and veterans' issues in order to provide culturally competent services; by recognizing the role of culture and military experience on the presentation of symptoms and make determinations on the most effective practices. The exploration into this frame of reference provides the necessary backdrop to guide professionals in helping veterans make meaning out of their various experiences while they were in military service. Being able to reconcile moral and ethical questions such as, "why they did what they did" with civilian perceptions with regards to this question, is often a source of confusion and frustration for troubled veterans. The inability to come to terms with these types of questions can impede their successful reintegration into American civilian society. Additionally, veterans need to re-formulate their military identity (i.e., as Soldier, Marine, Sailor, Airman) to encompass a new civilian role.

This primer was developed around a set of typical issues relating to veterans and military culture that are often addressed by human service professionals. The issues are presented here as topics with the more fundamental topics being addressed first.

It is useful to begin a discussion of service members' and veterans' issues with a self-assessment of the reader's general level of knowledge regarding the U.S. military. The self-assessment also contains questions regarding the reader's values and beliefs in relation to military policy. The reader is encouraged to take a few minutes to complete the following self-assessment. The answers to these questions relating to the U.S. armed forces will be discussed throughout the remaining pages.

Military Organization

Components of the U.S. Military

Conventional Forces

Since the advent of the Department of Defense's total force policy that went into effect in 1973, the U.S. military or armed forces is comprised of five service branches: Air Force, Army, Coast Guard, Marines, Navy and their respective reserve units: Air Force National Guard and the Army National Guard. The Reserves and National Guard units are trained to be "combat ready" but are not deployed in times of peace. The National Guard is the only part of the armed forces that is under both state and federal control, and the Coast Guard is currently resides under the Department of Homeland Security.

The Privatized Military

One of the prevailing assumptions that most civilians have about modern warfare is that it is carried out exclusively by military personnel who fight on behalf of the state for national security, self defense or for some other political cause. However, this is not actually the case. Until relatively recently, wars between sovereign states were fought to a large degree by for-profit contract forces. It was not until the twentieth century that the rise of the state system and the emergent concept of state sovereignty that norms against private arms began to develop (Singer, 2004).

The historical name for members of private armies is mercenaries. Historically, mercenaries have been mostly comprised of former soldiers who have been placed individually into various combat units for a particular client, and then they engage in combat for-pay for that client. Traditional mercenary activity has been banned by international law but it still persists throughout the world in a different form and with a different name. The new name for mercenaries is "civilian contractors." These private armies in the U.S. are either known as private military corporations (PMC) or privatized military firms (PMF). It is important to realize that this is more than a cosmetic change; it represents a fundamental change in how private armies are organized, staffed and operated.

PMF's are profit- driven organizations that trade in the provision of military services, but unlike their historical predecessors, their members are not all former soldiers and the services they provide do not just involve combat duties. Services also include strategic planning, intelligence gathering and analysis, operational support, troop training and military technical assistance (2001/2002). These modern organizations are organized hierarchically into incorporated and registered businesses that trade and compete openly on the international market; link to outside financial holdings, recruit more proficiently than their predecessors and provide a wider range of military services to a greater variety and number of clients. They openly publicize their services, have web sites and can be contacted by anyone with a cell phone or access to the Internet. Corporate structure is not the only distinguishing factor that sets PMF's apart from past private military ventures; these modern enterprises offer both efficiency and effectiveness and make use of complex corporate financing ranging from the sale of stock shares to intra-firm trading and thus can engage in a wide variety of deals and contracts.

As noted earlier, PMF's are not a new phenomenon in warfare, but the proliferation of PMF firms and the tremendous surge in PMF activity during the last ten years is a new occurrence (Singer, 2004). PMFs` currently operate all over the world and have influenced the outcomes of numerous conflicts such as the wars in Angola, Croatia, Ethiopia-Eritrea and Sierra Leone (Singer). They work with other corporations as well as with 3rd world countries and highly industrialized nations, including the United States. In fact, every major U.S. military operation in the post-Cold War era has involved significant levels of PMF support. Military operations such as those in Bosnia, Haiti, Kosovo, Somalia, or Zaire were all supported prominently by PMF involvement. The U.S. military has also employed PMF's to perform a range of services from recruiting, to military instruction in ROTC (Reserve Officers' Training Corps – college based officer commissioning programs), to training law enforcement.

Basic PMF Categories

Privatized military firms are typically divided into three broad categories: military provider firms, military consulting firms and military support firms (Singer, 2004). However, there are some firms such as MPRI (Military Professional Resources Inc.) that are capable of rendering services across categories. Military provider firms are most like the historical private armies in that they provide services in the battle zone by engaging in actual combat, or by directing and controlling other field units.

These firms are most likely to be hired by clients who have low military capabilities and who are facing immediate high-threat situations (Singer). In addition to MPRI, other notable military service provider firms include: Airscan, Blackwater (now XE), Executive Outcomes and Sandline.

Military consulting firms essentially provide advisory and training services. The main task of these firms is to provide the information and resources necessary to improve the management and training of the client's military forces. Unlike military provider firms, military consulting firms do not actually engage in combat. They advise, inform, and train the military personnel who actually do the fighting. The clients of this type of organization are not typically facing immediate threat; rather, they are interested in upgrading their military forces. Contracts with military consulting firms, therefore, tend to be longer and more profitable for the firm. Notable military consulting firms include: Levdan, MPRI, and Vinnell (Singer, 2004).

Military support firms do not participate in combat, in the planning of operations, or the training of combatants. They provide logistics, technical support, transportation, engineering and other rear-echelon services critical to the support of military operations. The clients of these firms are typically engaged in immediate and long term interventions (Singer, 2004). Military support firms are typically born out of a parent corporation expanding its service into the military market; notable in this category is Halliburton, which originally focused on domestic construction projects in the private sector and now has switched to military engineering projects (Avant, 2005).

Issues Related to the Use of PMF's in Current U.S. Military Operations

There are currently approximately 180,000 civilian contract personnel in the various war zones of the Middle East (Miller, 2007b). Although there have always been civilian personnel employed in major U.S. military operations, this large number of civilian personnel in current war zones pose several unique problems to the military and in negatively influencing the world's opinion of the U.S. For example, the presence of PMF employees, who are often thought of as support personnel for U.S. troops, may actually contribute to decreased morale among conventional U.S. service members. Employees of PMF's often perform the same duties as regular service members but receive substantially more salary with better benefits than the regular troops. They are often better equipped than regular U.S. military forces and have more frequent opportunities for R&R (rest and relaxation). In addition, because these combatants are employees of corporations they are essentially free from the constraints of the chain of command and the military rules of engagement. Thus, these freedoms result in greater flexibility and selectivity in the assignments they carry out as well as the times and conditions under which they carry them out.

The increased presence of PMF employees may have contributed to the increasingly negative perception of U.S. military personnel abroad. In most instances PMF employees are indistinguishable in appearance from regular

U.S. military personnel. They work in the same environments, wear the same clothing, and very often carry out the same functions including tactical operations. However, because they are civilian employees rather than members of the U.S. military and have not taken an oath of loyalty to the U.S. government, they do not necessarily share the military values and precepts of U.S. troops. Their on-duty and off-duty behavior is much less prescribed than the behavior of regular troops and not influenced by military standards or by the military code of ethics. Hence many of the instances of unprofessional conduct or human rights violations that are attributed to U.S. military personnel have actually been carried out by members of PMF's.

Additionally, since PMF's are corporations, this may present a conflict of interest between economics advantage and political agenda (Singer, 2004). For instance, the client's support or security objectives and the corporation's goal of maximizing profits can sometimes be at odds. Hence, PMF's can be tempted to cut corners or to overcharge for services to increase profits. The profit motive increases the likelihood that PMF's will prolong their contracts and avoid risks to their corporate assets (Singer, 2004).

In order to illustrate the corporate dilemmas that have been brought forth, the discussion will turn to two civilian contractors, DynCorp and Halliburton. DynCorp is one of the oldest PMF's in the U.S. and it is not free from controversy. It began in 1946 as a collaborative business venture by a small group of World War II pilots who sought to use their military contacts to make a living in the air freight business. DynCorp was originally called California Eastern Airways and landed a contract to deliver supplies to Asia during the Korean War (Miller, 2007b). By 2002, DynCorp was the nation's 13th largest military contractor with nearly $2.3 billion in annual revenue. In 2009, DynCorp received an estimated 117 million in military related contracts. From January through July 2010, they were awarded 80 million in such contracts (Department of Defense, 2010a).

DynCorp is based in Reston, Virginia and is typically recognized in the United States as a major supplier of private security officers for shopping malls and office buildings. However, DynCorp has a much broader and multinational range of services. DynCorp employees comprise the core of the current police force in Bosnia, while DynCorp pilots and their planes fly defoliation missions over the coca crops in Columbia (Scahill, 2005). DynCorp troops provide security for Afghan president Hamid Karzai and are also in charge patrolling the border posts between the U.S. and Mexico. The company runs many of the Department of Defense's weapons testing ranges and also reviews security clearance applications of civilian and military personnel for the U.S. Navy (Scahill).

In 2003, the U.S. State Department awarded DynCorp a multimillion-dollar contract to advise the Iraqi government on how to set up effective law enforcement, judicial, and correctional agencies. DynCorp agreed to send up to 1,000 civilian law enforcement experts to Iraq to train, help, and mentor local officials at the municipal, provincial, and national levels (Scahill, 2005). This PMF also agreed to provide the logistical and technical support necessary for this peacekeeping project. DynCorp estimates profits of approximately $50 million for the first year of the contract (Scahill).

The controversy associated with the U.S. government utilizing the services of a private contractor such as DynCorp arises from a variety of sources. The primary source deals with the rationale for why the U.S. military is privatizing military operations. Why is a PMF being used to carry out military objectives? What makes a PMF more qualified to carry out a military mission than the most technologically sophisticated military force on earth? It is difficult for the average U.S. citizen to generate philosophically compelling answers to these questions. For many, it is easier to speculate cover-ups, conspiracies, and unscrupulous motives the U.S. military does not wish to acknowledge.

The second major cause of controversy involves the questionable professional conduct of some DynCorp employees. For instance, in 2001 a group of Ecuadorian peasants filed a suit against DynCorp claiming that the defoliants they sprayed in Columbia drifted into Ecuador destroying their legitimate crops, causing illness in livestock, and even killing children. No action was taken against DynCorp since the Assistant Secretary of State intervened on behalf of the firm because the lawsuit posed a threat to U.S. national security and foreign policy objectives. During the same year, Kathryn Bolkovac, a U.N. International Police Force monitor filed suit against DynCorp for firing her after she reported that DynCorp police trainers in Bosnia were engaging in weapons and human trafficking (including child prostitution); as a result, many DynCorp employees were subsequently forced to resign but none were prosecuted because they enjoyed immunity from prosecution in Bosnia (Scahill, 2005).

Halliburton is the largest oil and gas services company in the world and is also one of the most controversial corporations in the United States. In 2005, Halliburton was the largest corporate benefactor of the war in Iraq making over $18 billion dollars thus far in contracts to restore Iraq's oil industry and to support U.S. troops (Scahill, 2005). Kellogg, Brown, and Root (KBR), a former subsidiary of Halliburton, was awarded more than $16 billion in government contracts for work in Iraq and Afghanistan from 2004-2006 (Collaborative Research on Organizations, 2009). Although Halliburton sold KBR in 2007, the company profited greatly from KBR's government contracts and continued to profit from the wars in Iraq and Afghanistan (Huffington, 2010).

Halliburton is not as old as DynCorp, yet it is also not new to government contracts. From 1962 to 1972 the U.S. Department of Defense paid Halliburton tens of millions of dollars to work in South Vietnam building roads, landing strips, harbors, and military bases (Scahill). In the early 1990s the company was awarded a contract to study and implement the privatization of routine military functions on behalf of then-Secretary of Defense Dick Chaney. Halliburton's findings suggested that the contracting-out of military services would result in substantial savings on military expenditures. When Mr. Chaney resigned as Secretary of Defense, he became CEO of Halliburton. Mr. Chaney was very successful in increasing government contracts to Halliburton, including a $2.2 billion contract to support U.S. troops in the Balkans, until 2000 when he resigned as CEO to become Vice President of the United States (Scahill).

Brown and Root, Halliburton's parent company, reported that Halliburton generated approximately $13 billion dollars in 2001 as a result of military contracts. Brown and Root was paid $16 million by the U.S. government to build a 408-person prison for captured Taliban fighters in Guantanamo Bay, Cuba. Although Halliburton has been very successful in securing government contracts for military support, it has also been accused of fraud, waste, and corruption; more than any other civilian contractor in Iraq (Scahill).

Independent agencies are still skeptical regarding the claimed financial savings from outsourcing military support operations. According to the Government Accounting Office (GAO), a study in February 1997 indicated that the Brown and Root operation in Bosnia that was estimated to cost $191.6 million when presented to Congress in 1996 had actually swollen to $461.5 million dollars by 1997 (Scahill). Brown and Root has also been investigated for unscrupulous domestic operations and paid $2 million dollars to settle a suit with the U.S. Justice Department for alleged cost overruns.

DynCorp and Halliburton are both exemplars of some of the major concerns regarding the U.S. military's collaborative partnerships with PMF's. The question of cost effectiveness continues to be an issue and as well their level of professionalism and the lack of public trust. At one time U.S. diplomats and military personnel were the primary agents of U.S. foreign policy; since the expanded role of PMF's in the modern warscape this is no longer the case. The question of who is responsible and who is in command is more complex than ever. The current state of affairs with regards to the privatization of military services cannot help our troops or the people that sacrifice their lives to help. The current military presence in occupied countries no longer represents the values, discipline, and cultural ethos of U.S. service members. Yet another example of questionable practices lie with the PMF, Blackwater International, (now called XE) and the controversial occupation of Iraq.

The final issue related to the number of PMF employees in the Middle East has a particular relevance for counselors and other mental health professionals. The presence of such large numbers of PMF employees in the war zone creates at least two new categories of clients who may have experienced combat related trauma. First, there are the hundreds of civilian personnel that may return from their war zone assignments with combat - induced stress disorders including PTSD. Many of these potential clients will have been armed combatants but others will be truck drivers or cafeteria workers who came under fire and/or witnessed acts of massive destruction and loss of human life. Unlike their military counterparts, this particular group of combat "veterans" will not be eligible for services from the Department of Veterans Affairs. They will not be able to seek assistance at Vet Centers. They will only be able to see civilian therapists (with private insurance) for help with their complaints. Secondly, there will be those military personnel who left the military and joined a PMF because they either could not successfully readjust to civilian life or because they found combat to be the main activity that gave their lives meaning. Unfortunately, it is unlikely that counselors or other mental health professionals will see clients from this second category. The reason being is that it is very likely that these veterans are already suffering from the negative consequences of war zone stress reactions, but they are the ones that will least likely seek help. However, it is very likely that counselors and other mental health professionals will see clients from the first category either individually or as participants in family or couples counseling. This need underscores the importance of having a large number of civilian therapists who are prepared to work with clients who suffer from war zone-induced PTSD.

Eligibility for the Military Service

Military service in the U.S. armed forces has typically been open to anyone who is an American citizen, between the ages of 18 and 35, with a high school diploma, without a criminal record and in relatively good health. However, there are a few exceptions and variations in these guidelines. First, American citizenship is not actually necessary to serve in the U.S. armed forces. Military service is open to anyone who is a legal resident of the United States. This means that resident aliens (green card holders) are eligible to serve in the U.S. military. One of the myths regarding resident aliens serving in the military is that it accelerates the process for citizenship. This very rarely happens and when it does, it typically takes place only during times of war.

Second, even though the legal age to enter the armed forces is 18, individuals who obtain signed consent from their parents or legal guardians may enter at age 17. Also individuals who wish to enter Officer Candidate School (OCS) must be no more than 32 when they enter military service. Third, although the high school diploma is a requirement for entry into the military, recruits that hold the General Education Diploma (GED) may have to complete additional requirements.

Fourth, "relatively good health" means freedom from a wide variety of common medical and psychological disorders. For example recruits who are obese or who are insulin dependent will not be accepted into the military. Another example is that if individuals have had a previous diagnosis of ADD or ADHD, they must verify that they have been able to function without medication for at least one month prior to entering military service. They must also demonstrate that they can perform satisfactorily through boot camp without the need for prescribed medication.

Finally, individuals who identify themselves as gay, lesbian, or bisexual are barred from military service. The official policy of the Department of Defense and Public Law 103-160, Section 654, Title 10 passed in 1993 is that homosexuals are excluded from military service. Although past president Clinton sought to lift the ban on gays serving in the military and also sought to accommodate gays in the military through his "Don't Ask, Don't Tell (DADT) Policy," congress never officially approved that policy. The rationale was that the concept of DADT was unworkable and indefensible in court (Center for Military Readiness, 2002). Public Law 103-106 essentially codified the language that had been present in Department of Defense regulations since 1981. The law states that:

> The prohibition against homosexual conduct is a long standing element of military law. The presence of persons who demonstrate a propensity or intent to engage in homosexual acts would create an unacceptable risk to the high standards of morale, good order, and discipline and unit cohesion that are the essence of military capacity

Some believe that, homosexuality can have negative effects on soldier's discipline, morale, and overall combat readiness. The statute further directs that any member of the armed services that engages in homosexual conduct or that indicates a propensity to engage in such conduct by stating that he or she is homosexual or bisexual or using other words to that effect shall be separated from the armed forces (PL103-160, 1993).

Currently, recruiters no longer ask potential inductees if they engage in or have engaged in homosexual behavior, and this may give some gay inductees the impression that the "Don't Ask, Don't Tell" policy and its variation, the "Don't ask, don't tell, don't pursue, and don't harass" policy have the effect of law. However, this is not the case. Service members who engage in homosexual behaviors, including soliciting others to engage in homosexual acts, regardless of whether the behavior takes place on base or off base or on duty or off duty, will be, with rare exceptions, discharged from the military (Center for Military Readiness, 2002).

According to the Service members Legal Defense Network (2010), more than 13,500 service members have been discharged since 1994 under this policy. Women and young adults between the ages of 18-25 seem to be disproportionately affected by the policy (Service members Legal Defense Network, 2010). For example, though women made up 15% of the Armed forces in 2002, they represented 36% of the discharges, and while women constituted 7% of the Coast Guard, they accounted for 34% of the discharges. Women seem to be particularly affected due to a phenomenon known as "lesbian baiting." In lesbian baiting, a woman is identified as a lesbian in retaliation for a poor performance review, or for refusing a man's sexual advances or after reporting a man for sexual harassment. Young adults are also affected disproportionately. In 2002, 83% of those discharged from the Air Force due to questions about sexual orientation were between the ages of 18-25 though they account for only 35% of the population of the Air Force.

The "don't harass" part of the policy does not seem to be helping either. A 2002 Defense Department inspector general survey showed that 80% of service members had heard offensive speech, derogatory names, jokes, or remarks about gay service members in the preceding year. Thirty seven percent reported witnessing or directly experiencing targeted forms of harassment including verbal and physical assaults and property damage. Overwhelmingly, service members did not report these types of harassment for fear of retaliation.

Registration for military service for young men is still compulsory, but military service is not compulsory at this time. The draft (conscription) ended in 1973, and since that time, military service in the U.S has been voluntary. Those who enlist typically agree to an eight year commitment with two to six years of active duty. However, it is possible to end active duty in as few as two years. At that point, many of these soldiers elect to join the Reserves or the National Guard to finish out their commitment. Those that do not choose either of these options finish out their time in the Individual Ready Reserve. This group, which is comprised of former soldiers, are not eligible to receive pay and do not train, but they do get points toward military retirement (Davey, 2004). Although the Individual Ready Reserve is very seldom activated, soldiers in this group can be called back to active duty at any time until their commitment expires. Further, the commitment for officers in the Individual Ready Reserve does not expire until they formally resign their commissions. This means that male and female officers in their late 40s could be called back to duty if needed.

In many other countries, military service for men is still compulsory and in others it is compulsory for women as well. The main advantage of conscription is that it guarantees a predetermined number of trained and combat ready soldiers. In the absence of conscription, large numbers of men and women must be persuaded to join the military, and that is the primary responsibility of military recruiters. Military recruiters are typically active duty personnel from the various service branches who are assigned the task of recruiting others into military service. Each recruiter has a certain target number of recruits for each month. Those who do not meet their quotas run the risk of receiving poor performance ratings and even loss of rank. The recruitment position is usually time limited.

Recruiting expenditures for the all-volunteer force was approximately 1.8 billion dollars in 1996 or an average of about $5,400 per enlisted recruit, and it rose to approximately $11,600 per recruit in the 1990s (Hellinger & Judd, 1991). The budget for recruitment advertising rose from $216 million annually in 1986 to $265 million annually in 2000 (Jaffe, 2000). In 2005 the Marine Corps, Navy, Air Force, and Army spent an estimated $431.8 million on recruiter support and $454 on advertising. Respectively the Marine Corps spent an estimated $4.9 million on recruiter support and $3 million on advertising costs; the Navy 75.9 and 112.3; the Air Force 50.4 and 54.9; the Army 300.6 and 283.8 (Congressional Budget Office, 2006).

During the 1990s military recruitment was relatively successful. However, this is no longer the case. As of May, 2005, the Army had attracted 35,926 new recruits, less than half of the October goal of 80,000 new recruits for 2005. This shortfall in new recruits has caused the military to cancel leaves and extend the tours of duty for service members already in the war zone. The military has also activated the Individual Ready Reserves. Although this is a very sizeable pool of soldiers (approximately 110,000), the majority of them have not worn a uniform, held a weapon, or trained for many years (Davey, 2004). Approximately half of the first group of 4,000 that were notified to return to active duty are asking for exemptions due to hardships such as illness, single parenthood, and financial troubles. Further, a smaller group of soldiers have filed lawsuits making the claim that they are no longer eligible for service (Davey). Recruitment seems to be in crisis. The wars in Afghanistan and Iraq, the current war on terrorism and the necessity for an ever increasing number of U.S. troops may reopen the discussion on the need for conscripted service in the U.S.

Reasons for Joining the Military

Men and women join the military for a variety of reasons. Some join because of the opportunities for travel and adventure. Others join out of family tradition. Still others join out of a sense of patriotism. There are those who join because they are undecided about their plans after high school and view military service as a way to learn professional skills and start a career path while saving money for college through the GI Bill. However, the GI Bill of 2005 is not the same as the original GI Bill of 1944.

The original GI Bill provided returning veterans of World War II with education benefits, unemployment checks, and home loan guarantees. Tuition, books and fees were fully covered at any college or job-training program, public or private, in the U.S. The Post 9/11 GI Bill covers only about 70 percent of the cost of attending a four-year public institution (Farrell, 2005), with a fixed annual stipend of $1000 for books and supplies with stipulations based on enrollment. It also includes a monthly housing allowance based on a Basic Allowance for Housing scale, location of the school attending, and presence of dependants (Department of Veterans Affairs, 2010e).

The Post 9/11 GI Bill became effective for training on or after August 1, 2009, and will pay tuition based upon the highest in-state public tuition charged by an educational institution in the state where the educational institution is located. The Yellow Ribbon Program may cover additional costs if the service member is attending a private institution, graduate school, or attending in an out-of-state status, and if the institution voluntarily enters into an agreement with the VA (Department of Veterans Affairs, 2010g). With the passing of this bill, for the first time in history service members are able to transfer unused educational benefits to their spouses or children (Department of Veterans Affairs, 2010g).

For many, another traditional reason for joining the military is that it is a guaranteed employer with equal opportunities for pay and advancement as well as offering excellent benefits for service members and their families.

Women join the military for the same reasons that men join. Also the advent of the all- volunteer force removed the 2% quota that had restricted the number of women who could serve as active duty in the military. It also increased the number of career opportunities open to women as well (Pilkington, 2010). Today approximately 15% of the active duty force includes women, and of the approximately 378,500 enlisted women servicing as active duty, 39.5% are minorities.

The Veteran Population

The U.S census defines a veteran as someone 18 or older who is not currently on active duty but who once served as active duty in the Army, Air Force, Coast Guard, Marine Corps, or Navy, or who served in the Merchant Marine during World War II (U.S. Census Bureau, 2003). This definition refers to people who served for only a short time or to those who served for many years and it does not distinguish between those who served in times of peace or in times of war.

A large number of veterans currently live in the U.S., but their number has continued to decline during the last twenty years. In 1980 28.5 million veterans lived in the U.S; this number declined to 27.5 million in 1990. According to the 2000 U.S. Census, there were approximately 26.4 million veterans living in the United States, which was 12.7% of the adult population. The primary reason for the consistent decline in the number of veterans in the U.S. is the continued aging and death of veterans from World War I, World War II, and the Korean War during the last twenty years (U.S. Census Bureau, 2003).

Vietnam era veterans, 8.4 million, accounted for the largest populations of veterans in 2000. Nearly 33% of all living veterans are from the Vietnam Era. World War II veterans make up the next largest group with approximately 5.7 million members or 21.7% of all veterans. There are no longer any living veterans from the Civil War but there are living veterans from every other major U.S. military conflict.

Although the number of male veterans has declined, the number of women veterans has continued to increase. Approximately 10% of veterans who served from May 1975 to August 1980 were women and approximately 13% of those who served from September 1980 to July 1990 were women (U.S. Census Bureau, 2003). From August 1990 to present, approximately 15% of veterans have been women. The median age for veterans living in the U.S. in 2000 was 57.4 years. The median age ranged from 33.3 years for those serving since August 1990 to 76.7 years for veterans of World War II (U.S. Census, 2003). During this period, approximately 9.7 million veterans were over 65 and 16.7 million were over 65 (U.S. Census Bureau, 2003).

Women in the Military

Women did not officially become a part of the armed forces until 1901 when the U.S. Army established the Army Nurses Corps; at this point the participation of women in the armed forces had been very prescribed and restricted to primarily supportive roles. They have served as cooks, tailors, and nurses and sometimes as couriers, scouts, and even spies because women had been expressly forbidden to be armed combatants. Today, it is not unusual to see women at the front lines or serving as pilots in helicopters and other aircraft.

In 2009 there were 208,829 women, or 14.3% of service members, serving on active duty in the U.S. military. In addition, women compose 17.7% of reserve members, and 15.1% of the National Guard (Women in Military Service for America

Memorial Foundation, 2009). About 10% of U.S. forces serving in Iraq and Afghanistan are women (Department of Veterans Affairs, 2010b). Women veterans are also the fastest growing segment of the veteran population, second only to elderly veterans. Currently, approximately 1.8 million women veterans comprise eight percent of the total veteran population. States with the largest number of women veterans are California, Texas, Florida, Virginia, and Georgia (Center for Women Veterans, 2010). With the increasing number of women service members, it is estimated that by 2020 women veterans will comprise 10% of the total veteran population (Medical News Today, 2008).

Although women veterans are entitled to the same VA and Department of Defense benefits as their male counterparts, some of them often face unique challenges and conditions as they attempt to make the transition from military to civilian status that are different from those of their male counterparts. Many of these challenges and risks arise from their status as primary care providers for children. Two of these challenges include: increased risk for loss of medical insurance and increased risk for homelessness (The American Legion Guide, 2008).

Upon discharge from the military, most veterans lose their health care coverage, but they are eligible to apply to the VA. However, the VA does not provide health care for dependent children or for the spouses of veterans. Consequently, women veterans who are primary caregivers will need to apply for the Tricare family plan or some other form of insurance if they are not able to secure medical benefits from a civilian employer. While this type of health insurance is available, it is not affordable for many women veterans who are also single parents.

Another issue is the risk of homelessness. Women veterans may be more at risk for homelessness because of the lack of financial and emotional support they may encounter when they make the transition to civilian life. Since women are likely to be to be the primary care providers for their children, if they have difficulties securing or maintaining housing, they and their children are at risk for homelessness. Also, women veterans seeking shelter from abusive relationships are at risk for becoming homeless. In addition, substance abuse plus a history of domestic violence places many women veterans at heightened risk for incarceration and resulting homelessness, because some of the risks they take for their survival and for the survival of their children may also be illegal (The American Legion Guide, 2008). Although the vast majority of women veterans do complete the transition to civilian life successfully, it is important to note that others do not.

A final issue is the risk of incarceration. Substance abuse and a history of violence also place many women veterans at risk for incarceration because the risks they take may also be illegal.

Women veterans tend to commit crimes and take risks related to the survival of themselves and their children (The American Legion Guide). This is clearly not to say that all women veterans will have difficulties with transitioning to civilian life.

Geographic Dispersion

The largest population of veterans in the United States (9.9 million) lives in the South (9.9 million) and in the Midwest (6.1 million) (U.S. Census Bureau, 2003). The South also has the largest proportion of veterans in the adult population (13.4%) of the region. The West has the next largest population of veterans (5.7 million) and the Northeast has the smallest veteran population with 4.6 million members. The state with the largest number of veterans is California, with over 2.5 million. Six other states (Florida, Texas, New York, Pennsylvania, Ohio, and Illinois) have veteran populations of one million or more (U.S. Census Bureau, 2003). Nevada is the state with the fastest growing veteran population, with the population increasing from 182,000 to 238,000 between 1990 and 2000 (U.S. Census Bureau, 2003).

Alaska is the state with the largest percentage of the state population comprised of veterans with 17.1%. The lowest percentages of veterans in the adult population are in New York (9.5%) and the District of Columbia (9.8%). Non-metropolitan and rural counties in the U.S. had the largest concentrations of veterans in 2000. However, Florida may be an exception due to retiree migration (U.S. Census Bureau, 2003). Six of the ten places with the highest concentrations of veterans are in Virginia, and the greatest concentration of veterans (27.1%) is in Hampton, Virginia (U.S. Census Bureau, 2003). One reason for this is that the largest U.S. naval station is also in that area. Hampton is followed by Clarksville, Tennessee (24.4%) and Fayetteville, N.C. (23%). With the exception of Colorado Springs, Colorado, the home of the U.S. Air Force Academy, all of the places of highest concentrations of veterans are in the South (U.S. Census Bureau, 2003).

Employment

The majority of veterans living in the U.S. (54.7%) continued to participate in the civilian workforce during 2000. The largest veteran cohort that was employed was the group that served from September 1980 to July 1990 and reported as having 82.7% employment. The second largest cohort was comprised of veterans who served from August 1990 forward with 81.4%. More than 75% of veterans from the Vietnam era were employed during 2000 and more than half (51.4%) of those who served from July 1955 to July 1964 were employed. The rate of employment for Korean War veterans and World War II veterans were relatively low with rates of 24.6% and 11.6% respectively. A significant proportion of the veterans from the Vietnam Era and prior will have retired. Given the relative high rates of employment in 2000, only 5.6% of veterans lived below the poverty level compared with 10.9% of the civilian adult population in the U.S. The youngest veterans, those who served from August 1990 forward, were the veterans that were most likely to be poor with a poverty rate of 6.2% while the poverty rate for Vietnam era veterans during the same period was 5.1% (U.S. Census Bureau, 2003).

In 2009, the Department of Veterans Affairs issued the 2009 Community Homelessness Assessment, Local Education and Networking Groups (CHALENG) Report, which estimated that 107,000 veterans are homeless on any given night (National Coalition for Homeless Veterans, 2010). It has also been reported that approximately one-third of homeless adults in the United States are veterans. Iraq and Afghanistan veterans represent approximately 1.8% of the homeless veteran population. The number of homeless Vietnam era veterans is estimated to exceed the number of fatalities that occurred during the war (Foster, 2010).

Race and Ethnicity

The ethnic and racial composition of veterans has begun to more closely resemble the general population as a whole. About 72 % of the U.S. adult population was White in 2000 and the proportion of White veterans was approximately 83%. The second largest veteran group was African American representing 9.7% of veterans, and during 2000, African Americans accounted for a little more than 11% of the U.S. population. Other racial and ethnic groups show similar trends (U.S. Census Bureau, 2003). The smallest percentages of the veteran populations were American Indians and Alaska Natives with 0.7% followed by Native Hawaiians and other Pacific Islanders at 0.1 % (U.S. Census Bureau, 2003).

Military Issues Self-Assessment
Military Branches and Structure

1. Military Pay Grades (E-levels) and rank are equivalent   T   F

2. Private First Class in the Army is a higher rank than Private First Class in the Marines   T   F

3. The Navy and the Coast Guard do not have the rank of Sergeant.   T   F

4. An E-5 in the Army and an E-5 in the Coast Guard earn the same base salary.   T   F

5. The rank of Lance Corporal is only found in the Marines   T   F

6. Second Lieutenant is the first (lowest) commissioned officer grade of the Army, Air Force and Marines.   T   F

7. All service branches have the rank Captain   T   F

8. The rank of Major is above Captain and Lieutenant in the Army, Marines, and Air Force.   T   F

9. An Army sergeant, an Air Force staff sergeant, a Marine corporal, and a Navy petty officer third class are all considered to be NCO ranks.   T   F

10. All of the service branches have a Reserve and a National Guard Component.   T   F

11. The Navy is second only to the Air Force in the number of offensive aircraft and missiles it maintains   T   F

12. The Marines have no enlisted doctors, nurses, or medics.   T   F

Match the letter of the service branch with the words or statements that follow them.

A. Air Force
B. Army
C. Coast Guard
D. Marines
E. Navy

13. Historical mission is to assault, capture, and control "beach heads" through offensive amphibious deployment. _____

14. Mission includes deployment of aircraft where fixed runways are impossible . _____

15. Maintains responsibility for all U.S. strategic nuclear ballistic missiles _____

16. Was part of the Army until 1947. _____

17. Formerly under the Department of Transportation _____

18. Established in 1775 by the Continental Congress. _____

19. Provides maritime security for U.S. coasts, ports, and inland waterways. _____

20. Land combat and service forces trained for sustained combat in support of national security, objectives or policies. _____

21. Force Recon _____

22. SEALs _____

23. Rangers _____

24. Green Berets (Special Forces) _____

25. Delta Force _____

Answers to the self-assessment (Questions 1-25):

5. True	10. False	15. A	20. A	25. B
4. True	9. True	14. E	19. C	24. B
3. True	8. True	13. D	18. B and/or E	23. B
2. True	7. True	12. True	17. C	22. E
1. False	6. True	11. True	16. A	21. D

Military Culture and the Mission of the Military

Military Culture

Military culture is comprised of the values, beliefs, traditions, norms, perceptions and behaviors that govern how members of the armed forces think, communicate, and interact with one another as well as with civilians. This notion of culture also determines how military personnel view their function in life, their status, and the role of the military in American society. Thus, this discussion will begin with a focus on military values followed by military virtues.

Military Values

Each branch of the military has a set of core values that is somewhat different, yet similar in essence among all of the service branches. Values that are reflected in all of the service branches include honor, courage, loyalty, integrity, and commitment. The following sections will briefly discuss the meaning of these values as drawn from different branches of the armed services. The discussion is presented as a monologue spoken by a representative of a particular branch of service. The discussion begins with honor.

Honor: "I will bear true faith and allegiance..."

We will conduct ourselves in the highest ethical manner in all relationships with peers, superiors and subordinates; be honest and truthful in our dealings with each other, be willing to make honest recommendations and accept those of junior personnel.

We will encourage new ideas and deliver bad news, even when it is unpopular; abide by an uncompromising code of integrity, taking responsibility for our actions and keeping our word; and fulfill or exceed our legal and ethical responsibilities in our public and personal lives twenty-four hours a day. Illegal or improper behavior or even the appearance of such behavior will not be tolerated. We are accountable for our professional and personal behavior. We will be mindful of the privilege to serve our fellow Americans (U.S. Navy, 2009).

Integrity:

We demonstrate uncompromising ethical conduct and moral behavior in all of our personal actions. We are loyal and accountable to the public trust (U.S. Coast Guard, 2009).

Courage: "I will support and defend…"

We will meet the demands of our profession and the mission when it is hazardous, demanding, or otherwise difficult. We will make decisions in the best interest of the service and the nation, without regard to personal consequences, and meet these challenges while adhering to a higher standard of personal conduct and decency. Courage is the value that gives us the moral and mental strength to do what is right, even in the face of personal or professional adversity (U.S. Navy, 2009).

Commitment: "I will obey my orders…"

We will demand respect up and down the chain of command. We will care for the safety, professional, personal and spiritual well being of our people; show respect toward all people without regard to race, religion, or gender; and treat each individual with human dignity. We will be committed to positive change and constant improvement; and exhibit the highest degree of moral character, technical excellence, quality and competence in what we have been trained to do. The day-to-day duty of every man and woman is to work together as a team to improve the quality of our work, our people and ourselves (U.S. Navy, 2009).

Loyalty: "Semper Fidelis" ("Always Faithful"): Moto of the Marine Corps

We will be loyal to our nation, ensuring the resources entrusted to us are used in an honest, careful, and efficient way (U.S. Navy, 2009).

Respect:

We value our diverse work force. We treat each other with fairness, dignity, and compassion. We encourage individual opportunity and growth. We encourage creativity through empowerment. We work as a team (U.S. Coast Guard, 2009).

Devotion to Duty:

We are professionals, military and civilian, who seek responsibility, accept accountability, and are committed to the successful achievement of our organizational goals. We exist to serve. We serve with pride (U.S. Coast Guard, 2009).

The values of the military determine the behaviors that serve as the standards of conduct for military personnel. The standards of conduct for members of the armed forces regulate member's lives 24 hours each day every day of the week beginning the moment they enter military status and ending only when the service member is discharged or otherwise separated from the military. The standards of conduct apply whether the service member is on-base or off-base or on-duty or off-duty.

The military believes this pervasive application of standards of conduct is necessary because members of the armed forces must be ready at all times to be deployed anywhere in the world to a combat environment.

The list of military values presented here is not exhaustive. In addition, each branch of the armed forces discusses its values in a slightly different manner. The goal of this discussion was to present some of the values that all of the service branches seem to espouse. The Soldier's Creed of the U.S. Army delineates the essential values and standards of conduct of the U.S. armed forces. It is presented here in its entirety.

The Soldier's Creed

I am an American Soldier.

I am a Warrior and a member of a team. I serve the people of the United States and live the Army Values.

I will always place the mission first.

I will never accept defeat.

I will never quit.

I will never leave a fallen comrade.

I am disciplined, physically and mentally tough, trained and proficient in my warrior tasks and drills.

I always maintain my arms, my equipment and myself.

I am an expert and I am a professional.

I stand ready to deploy, engage, and destroy the enemies of the United States of America in close combat.

I am a guardian of freedom and the American way of life.

I am an American Soldier.

Military Virtues

Traditionally, civilians assume that military virtues only include attributes such as courage, boldness, loyalty, strength, and stamina. DeGeorge (1987) however, discusses three often-ignored virtues that he believes should also characterize the military professional. These are: peacefulness, restraint, and obedience. Peacefulness refers to the military preferring to maintain peace rather than waging war. Ironically, peacekeeping often involves waging a war, thus, from a civilian perspective there may be no perceptible difference between forms of military action. From the military perspective, however, there is a clear difference in motivations and goals. Hence, peacefulness also promotes the second virtue of restraint. DeGeorge (1987) notes, that restraint as a virtue may not seem consistent with the other traditional military virtues of courage and boldness, but it is perhaps an even more important virtue. Not only must the military professional exercise restraint in using his or her power for properly sanctioned purposes, he or she must also be expected to use restraint in carrying out operations. The exercise of restraint means that force must be directed toward the enemy and not toward civilians or other noncombatants.

Restraint is also "central to the notion of a just war" (DeGeorge, 1987, p.18). The "Just War Doctrine" is an integral aspect of American military philosophy. It asserts that war is to be a last resort to be pursued only when all peaceful alternatives have failed. It asserts that there must be a particular "just cause" that necessitates recourse of war and that the expected costs of the war, in terms of human life and destruction of property, should be a "proportionate price for the good to be achieved by defending the just cause (O'Brien, 1984, p. 59). The war must also be authorized by those having the right to commit the nation to war. However, not even a "just cause" may serve as the impetus for an offensive war (O'Brien).

Finally, the just war doctrine states that the use of force must be limited to attaining the "just cause" and should not be motivated by hatred or by a desire for revenge (O'Brien). Hence, the military virtues of peacefulness and restraint undergird and affirm the "just war" doctrine.

The final military virtue of obedience as conceived by DeGeorge (1987), is thought to be more complex than a simple compliance with a command. DeGeorge states that obedience is only a virtue when applied to legitimate orders coming from legitimate authorities and "provided that what they [authorities] command is not immoral" (p.22). The commander's moral obligation is to accomplish legitimate military objectives (the mission) while minimizing loss of life for those under his command, while avoiding unnecessary death and destruction to civilian populations on either side of the conflict (Viotti, 1987). Hence, a commander is not obligated to follow an order he or she deems to be either immoral or illegitimate. However, once an order is issued, it is unlikely that it will not be followed regardless of the receiving officer's personal opinions.

Obedience to the chain of command assures compliance through the ranks. Chain of command and other military precepts will be discussed in the following section. Cook (2004) states that it is important to note that there is a dynamic tension between the highest ideals of the military profession and the realities faced by the military; as servants of particular nations where political leadership and power are employed for less than noble purposes. The acknowledgement of this reality is often a point of disappointment and disillusionment for many military personnel. However, the aspirations that are at the foundation of military virtues are real and are taken very seriously. Service to others, self-discipline and self-sacrifice for a greater a purpose are the most noble of human values (Cook, 2004).

Military Precepts

Just as there are laws and regulations that dictate social behavior within a given culture, formal mandates and codes of conduct also exist within the military setting. Among the most significant of these are: Chain of Command, the Geneva Convention, Just War Doctrine, Rules of Engagement, and the Unified Code of Military Justice.

Chain of Command

Chain of Command refers to the succession of commanding officers from superior to subordinate through which command is exercised via orders. It settles all questions of authority and avoids clashes of personality through a hierarchical system in which everyone has a place in relation to the other (Waller, 1944). Orders come from the top down and never from the bottom up. Everyone is under orders and there can never be any doubt regarding who has the right to order whom to do what (Waller). This is the principle of organization that allows the military to conduct its mission. Implicit in the notion of chain of command is the belief that any order that comes from a superior is legitimate and that it is the duty of the subordinate to carry out that order without question. Although subordinates, including individual soldiers have the right to refuse to carry out an order that they believe is immoral, in practice they very seldom do this. Unit cohesion, group morale plus the inherent belief in the chain of command usually override dissention.

The Geneva Convention

The Geneva Convention is actually four different documents that are international agreements concerning how warfare should be conducted. These agreements consider matters such as the treatment of sick and wounded soldiers, the care of shipwrecked sailors, the treatment of prisoners of war, the use of various military weapons and the treatment of civilians during wartime. Generally speaking, U.S. service members typically abide by the terms of these conventions however, sometimes they do not. For a variety of reasons-- most often involving revenge or retaliation—some service members engage in behaviors that are inconsistent with their training, values, and indoctrination. Since most U.S. service members view behavior that is inconsistent with the Geneva Convention as dishonorable and immoral, those who have committed these acts may suffer from feelings of shame and guilt subsequent to their actions.

Just War Doctrine

As stated previously, the "just war doctrine" is an integral aspect of American military philosophy and culture. War is a last resort to be pursued only when all peaceful alternatives have failed, and there must be a particular "just cause" that necessitates recourse to war. The "just war doctrine" also asserts that the expected costs of the war in terms of human life and destruction of property should be a "proportionate price for the good to be achieved by defending the just cause" (O'Brien, 1984, p. 59). The war must also be authorized by those having the right to commit the nation to war. In the United States this means having Congressional approval. In actual practice, the President of the United States has great latitude in ordering the deployment of troops. However, not even a "just cause" may serve as the only stimulus for an offensive war (O'Brien, 1984). Finally, the "just war doctrine" states that the use of force must be limited to attaining the just cause and should not motivated by hatred or by a desire for revenge (O'Brien).

Current U.S. military policy may sometimes seem to be slightly at odds with the notion of the "just war" doctrine. Certain characteristics of the "war on terror" could be viewed as containing elements of an offensive war or a war motivated by revenge. Nonetheless, it is the belief in the "just war" doctrine that allows U.S. service members to affirm their actions and the actions of their comrades as just, moral, and necessary even when they involve killing human beings. This belief is what allows service members to follow the chain of command and dedicate themselves to the completion of the mission; this helps service members with the rationale of "we are right" and "they [the enemy] are wrong." It provides the guiding philosophy and moral vantage point for combatants to perceive themselves as "just warriors" and guardians of freedom. However, it does not insulate them from civilian opinions and critical perceptions regarding their actions.

Rules of Engagement

The Rules of Engagement (ROE) are the directives issued by military authorities that prescribe the circumstances and limitations under which U.S. forces will initiate combat with and/or continue combat engagement with enemy forces. The ROE are also known as the "law of war." In practice, for example, the ROE would determine when and under what circumstances American forces in a war zone can return enemy fire.

The ROE are simultaneously a source of pride and frustration for American service members and veterans. They are a source of pride because these rules represent professionally bound principles for behavior in combat as standards of honor and are consistent with the "just war" doctrine. They are also designed to reduce the risk of unnecessary death of both civilians and combatants. The ROE can also be a source of frustration for U.S. combatants. For example, the Rules of Engagement in combat are often determined by military personnel who are not in the immediacy of the war zone, and the information used to determine the ROE may no longer be accurate. Hence the ROE that is established to guide the execution of a mission may actually inhibit the unit's ability to complete its mission.

The second source of frustration reported by veterans is that modern-day opposing enemy forces do not seem to be bound by ROE (or a "just war" doctrine), yet they use their knowledge of U.S. troops' ROE to their advantage. Veterans have reported, for example, that unnecessary U.S. casualties sometimes resulted from a ROE that required U.S. troops to maintain a defensive position rather than to pursue and destroy an enemy force that was harassing them (O'Brien, 1984).

Uniform Code of Military Justice

The Uniform Code of Military Justice is a federal law enacted by Congress and is applicable to all U.S. military personnel worldwide. It has 144 articles that cover all aspects of behaviors relative to appropriate military conduct. A majority of the code addresses the consequences of inappropriate behaviors and the mechanisms by which military trials are conducted and the manner in which cases are decided. For instance,

Articles 77 are known as the "punitive code" and contain specific offenses that will result in a service member's court martial.

Chain of command, the Geneva Conventions, Rules of Engagement, and the Uniform Code of Military Justice embody the values and virtues of military culture. These determine what should be done and how it should be done as well as the penalties that will be applied as consequences of poor conduct. The U.S. military does not currently have a separate set of ethical standards of behavior, but if it were to adopt such a set of standards, these would probably be based upon the four precepts presented here.

In what ways does military culture differ from American civilian culture?

The distinct characteristics of civilian American culture include an emphasis on individuality, individual achievement, personal freedom and fluid social mobility. These characteristics are in stark contrast to the military culture's strict hierarchical social structure and emphasis on "the mission," the chain of command, and group solidarity in pursuit of the mission. Social status in the military is very clear; whereby, officers have higher status than enlisted personnel and both officers and enlisted personnel are further ordered in status according to rank. Duties, responsibilities, pay, living arrangements and social interactions are all determined by rank, and appropriate insignia displayed on the military uniform easily identifies rank. Superiors and subordinates are clearly delineated, and one's place in the social structure is never ambiguous. Another less obvious distinction among armed forces personnel is membership in either regular forces or elite forces. The elites are comprised of special operations teams found in each branch of the armed forces. These individual teams receive special accommodations, special duties, and extra pay for the high-risk nature of their operations. The elite forces are comprised of Army Rangers, Special Forces (Green Berets) and Delta Force from the Army; Air Force Special Operations Command from the Air Force; Marine Corps Special Operations Command (MARSOC) and Force Reconnaissance from the Marines; and Navy SEALS from the Navy.

The mission, not the individual, is paramount in military culture. Loyalty and obedience to the chain of command are much more valuable than personal freedom and individual achievement. However, individual achievement is important to the degree that it supports efficient and effective completion of the mission. The military philosophy is that individuality ignores the importance of the group achieving the mission and therefore disrupts harmony, threatens discipline and breeds chaos. It is the group acting as one mind that accomplishes military objectives. This does not mean that the military does not value intelligence, creativity, and personal initiative. On the contrary, these characteristics are highly valued. In the military way of thinking, once a decision has been made to pursue a certain course of action, all of the superior qualities aforementioned should be used in order to successfully complete the mission. Accordingly, much of the self-worth of a member of the armed forces flows from his or her belief in how effective he or she has been in supporting the group and completing his or her part of the mission. The primacy of the mission, the importance of the group, the chain of command, and the regimentation of daily living, are all of the elements that set military culture apart from civilian culture.

Perhaps the most salient difference between civilian culture and military culture, however, is that devotion to duty in the military also includes being willing to sacrifice one's life for one's country, for one's comrades, and even for unknown persons that service members have been sent to protect. Military personnel volunteer to serve society in the application of coercive and lethal force. They serve on terms of unlimited liability meaning they follow lawful orders in full recognition that they may die or be severely injured in fulfillment of those orders (Cook, 2004, p.74). This commitment has a profound impact on the worldview of service members. Service members develop a worldview that reflects the values of military culture and for this reason they often times feel out of place upon returning to civilian life. Readjustment for military personnel to civilian culture is not as simple as civilians might think. It involves much more than taking off the uniform. For many veterans, it means learning a new lifestyle, language and adapting to a new culture.

Could cultural differences account for the historical tension and emotional distance between members of the military and civilian society?

There are notable differences between military institutions/traditions and civilian institutions. Sometimes tensions rise from clashes between these two cultures. The difference in how civilians perceive the function of the military and how service members view themselves is one source of tension. The civilian perspective may be understood in terms of a customer and service provider relationship (Davenport, 1987). The clients of the military are the citizens of the nation, unlike other customer and service provider relationships; there is a greater psychological distance between the professional (i.e., military) and the client (i.e., society). Davenport (1987) suggests that this "remoteness" between the professional soldier and the civilian client arises from the fact that "service to the client is rendered best in the absences of the client" (p.8). It is very clear that the civilian population does not want wars waged anywhere close to where they reside.

The military holds an absolute monopoly on deadly force in American society. Hooker (2003) poses the following question: How to keep the military "strong enough to defend the state and subservient enough not to threaten it is the central question in civil-military relations" (p. 5). Although the civilian citizens of the U.S. have assigned the members of the military profession the power of legalized violence, there remains some ambivalence among civilian citizens about the military's use of power (Davenport, 1987). On one hand, civilians are relieved because they can exercise great power through the military without experiencing the personal risk of combat. On the other hand they are fearful that the military will not relinquish its power after the war has ended or perhaps even turn its power against them (Davenport). This dynamic is in large part responsible for the psychological distance between the military professional and the civilian client.

The tension generated in this relationship also serves to draw members of the military profession closer to each other (Davenport, 1987). Consequently, the military profession is bound by a sense of camaraderie that is almost "inherently anti-civilian" (Davenport, p.10).

The military perspective seems to focus on the cardinal principle of unit cohesion and the fact that military life is inherently different that civilian life. Unit cohesion means that the bonds of trust among individual service members that result in combat effectiveness are greater than the sum of combat effectiveness of any of the individual members. Hence, unit cohesion is one of the most critical elements in combat capability.

In summary, military life is fundamentally different from civilian life. Military society is characterized by its own laws, rules, customs and traditions, including numerous restrictions on personal behavior that would not be acceptable in the civilian world. Military culture does broadly conform to constitutional norms of individual rights and liberties, but "derives from the functional imperative [battlefield success] and...values collective over individual good" (Hooker, 2003, p.6).

Therefore the extraordinary responsibilities of the armed forces, the unique conditions of military service, and the critical role of unit cohesion require that the military community, while being subject to civilian control, exist as a separate specialized society (Davenport, 1987). Hence, as Davenport (1987) notes, it is civilian ambivalence about the military's power plus the military's obsession with unit cohesion that serves to keep both cultures in conflict. Hooker (2003), however, states that the psychological distance and so-called estrangement between military culture and civilian society have been exaggerated. He suggests that the large number of veterans and reservists that live and co-mingle in civilian society have contributed to a greater understanding both from a psychological perspective and physical proximity, between these two segments of the American population. Although military culture embraces and imposes a set of values that more narrowly restricts individual behavior, civilians seem to accept the military's rationale for having a "conservative outlook that emphasizes the group over the individual and organizational success over personal validation" (Hooker, p.16). Although the dynamic tensions that teeter between civilian and military cultures may be sub-optimal, "they are far from dangerous" (Hooker, p.16). Thus, what is most relevant for counselors to remember in working with veterans is the salience of group reference and group orientation in effective treatment planning with veterans.

What is the mission of the military?

The concept of "mission" is very important in working with military clients. Mission has two distinct meanings. The first has to do with a specific military operation to which a unit of military personnel has been assigned. The second has to do with a broader purpose of overall functions and roles.

The traditional view of the mission of the military is to wage wars of self-defense. Another consideration is that the mission of the military is to implement a country's foreign policy (DeGeorge, 1987). This means that the traditional view is morally justifiable only if the foreign policy it implements is morally justified (DeGeorge).

Since wars of aggression are usually considered to be immoral, the appropriate primary mission of the military should be to keep peace and to fight defensive wars (DeGeorge). According to Davenport (1987), the paramount duty of the U.S. military profession is to promote the safety and welfare of humanity. This duty, according to military law takes precedence over the duty towards the civilian citizens they serve because those civilians are only a portion of the human race (Davenport, pp.7-8). Miskel (2001) suggests that the overall mission of the U.S. military is to ensure regional stability, to promote productive worldwide relationships, to defend allies and "friends," and to fight wars when necessary. Cebrowski (2001) further notes that America's international status and global interests require that the armed forces have as their operating domain not only the "majority of the earth's surface, but also the skies and space above, the ocean depths below, and the electronic environment we think of as cyberspace" (p. 9).

Former President George W. Bush stated that there are certain universal principles that apply to all of human civilization. These principles are referred to as the "nonnegotiable demands of human dignity" (Zelikow, 2005). They are: (a) the rule of law, (b) limits on the power of the state, (c) respect for women, (d) private property, (e) free speech, (f) equal justice, and (g) religious tolerance (p.112).

All seven of these principles focus on the relationship of the individual to the state, and they do not specify any particular form of government that would or could produce these relationships. It is clear however, that monarchy, socialism, theocracy and communism have been excluded as contenders because of the demands related to limits of power of the state and the availability of private property. Many of the theoretical tenets of these forms of government violate these demands, therefore making them incompatible with the universal principals put forward by President Bush.

It is then not difficult to infer that democracy might be the government that is being suggested to best be able to uphold these principles. The doctrine of nonnegotiable demands of human dignity seems to underpin much of current U.S. foreign policy (at least in theory).

The U.S. national security objectives are directly related to U.S. foreign policy and although they have changed somewhat with the demise of the former Soviet Union, the following four objectives have remained constant:

1. to prevent the coercion of the U.S. or its allies and friends

2. to be capable of protecting the U.S. and U.S. citizens abroad

3. to maintain access to critical resources around the globe including petroleum

4. to encourage long-term political stability

The doctrine of nonnegotiable demands of human dignity, however, suggests that a fifth objective be added:

5. to support the global expansion of democracy and capitalism
    Although this objective was never stated directly, it is certainly implied, and probably inherently understood and approved by the majority of members of the armed forces. To summarize, the mission of the mo ern U.S. military, therefore, seems to be to:

    (a) protect American interests outside the U.S. including guaranteeing access to strategic commodities,

    (b) implement American foreign policy,

    (c) promote (and enforce) world stability, and

    (d) engage in military operations that support U.S. national security objectives.

The United States has interests in every region of the earth and in each region, the interests are strategic or vital (Cebrowski, 2001). The breadth, scope, complexity, and often paradoxical nature of U.S. interests abroad make it likely that the U.S. will always face opposition from other nations. Wars and other conflicts seem unavoidable as long as the U.S. remains committed to preserving its status and power abroad (Boot, 2002).

How does the military carry out its mission?

The complexity of the mission of the U.S. military dictates that the military must have a number of responses to the various situations that threaten national interests. One such response entails that the U.S. have continual deployment of Navy and Marine Corps units in waters that are adjacent to locations of interest to U.S. security and foreign policy. This practice is known as "forward presence" and has been a cardinal principle of strategic planning (Cebrowski, 2001). Forward presence alone, however, is not accorded the status it once had. Few countries seem to be willing to have U.S. forces stationed within their borders or in their adjacent waters.

Some types of aggression defy early detection because they are disguised as civil wars or revolutionary insurgencies, but these conflicts also have the potential to develop into full-scale wars (Barnett, Tovar, & Shultz, 1984). The armed forces, therefore, has had to develop special preemptive responses to "low-visibility" or "low intensity warfare." These responses are called "special operations." Special operations are defined as small-scale, clandestine, covert or overt operations of an unorthodox and frequently high-risk nature undertaken to achieve significant political or military objectives in support of foreign policy (Tugwell & Charters, 1984).

Special operations are characterized by subtlety, imagination, the discriminate use of violence, and by oversight at the highest levels (i.e., the Pentagon), and military and non-military personnel may be used in concert (Tugwell & Charters, 1984). Special operations may be further classified as combat rescue missions, counter insurgency operations, and peacekeeping operations. The principles of the "just war" doctrine are applied to special operations and requires that these operations do not support immoral / and or illegal regimes, nor provide support for warring parties during civil wars (O'Brien, 1984). In addition, special operations should not take the form of "military interventions" because they are contrary to the international law principle supporting the sovereign equality of states.

Special operations that involve counter insurgency and peacekeeping, however, are often thought of as "interventions in a foreign state." In the military sense, an intervention is the "extraordinary interference in the internal or external affairs of another state in a manner … [that] affects it's government's exercise of sovereignty and alters the normal relations between the parties involved" (O'Brien, 1984, p.62).

Historically, U.S. military strategists have provided four justifications for overriding the noninterference clause of international law. The first justification is the invitation to intervene by a besieged state. The second justification is intervention by right of treaty. In this case the U.S. military intervention would be based upon a prior agreement for mutual defense of the state in question. The third justification is the protection of the lives and property of U.S. citizens in foreign states. The final justification and the one that seems to best represent the principles of the "just war" doctrine is to undertake a humanitarian intervention in order to protect an indigenous people from its own government (O'Brien, 1984).

The importance of the concept of special operations for counselors is relevant for two basic reasons. First it helps counselors to understand how military culture interprets the use of force to carry out its mission. It helps to inform the civilian counselor's knowledge of the military worldview. Second, it illustrates that many veterans will have served in military operations that received very little or no media coverage. These operations were nonetheless dangerous and high-risk, and probably involved loss of life of both civilians and military personnel. Special operations fought by a small number of professional Americans soldiers are much more typical of American history than the global armed conflicts that most Americans think of as wars (Boot, 2002).

Most U.S. military operations are not classified as "wars." The last declared war that U.S. troops fought was World War II. This does not change the fact the troops are deployed, lives are lost, and traumatic events occur. The military personnel that participate in low intensity wars are as much combat veterans as those who were combatants during World War II and are just as likely to have similar reactions to the war-zone experience.

The actual war zone experience of U.S. troops in a military operation that is called "a war" or termed "a special operation" is likely to be the same, but the public perception and reaction to the conflict can be very different depending on how the conflict is portrayed in the media. In order to illustrate some of these differences in public perception the following section will compare the public response to a well-known and "popular" war versus three less well-known and less popular modern-day special operations.

A Good and Just War: World War II

World War II generally occupies the American public imagination as the greatest military conflict and victory of American history. It was a true "just war" declared against a clearly identified "Axis of Evil" that threatened the welfare of all of humanity. It was a classic struggle between the forces of Good and Evil. It was a war that the U.S. tried to avoid but was dragged into in response to a devastating "surprise attack "that nearly destroyed the U.S. Pacific fleet. It was a war that enjoyed significant public support in terms of political rhetoric, the mass media and civilian production of war materials. It was a war that had a specific beginning and an identifiable end. Most importantly it was a war that resulted in a decisive victory for the Allied forces led by the U.S. (first in Europe and then in Asia with the defeat of Japan). American troops were universally hailed as liberators and held in high esteem not only in the U.S. but worldwide as well.

The war ended as it should: Good triumphed over evil. American troops returned home as conquering heroes to an appreciative country, proud and loving families, and to an expanding post-war economy. Veterans' benefits were the best they had ever been and millions of veterans of all races took advantage of the GI Bill to pursue higher education, start businesses, and purchase homes. By the time the original GI Bill ended in 1956, 7.8 million WWII veterans had participated in an education or training program. From 1944 to 1952, the VA backed nearly 2.4 million home loans for World War II veterans (Department of Veterans Affairs, 2010d). This was a time of a "great leap forward" in American society. It was a triumph for democracy and the "American way of life" and a verification that "God was on our side." In every war since World War II, American soldiers and American citizens have tried to regain this feeling of supreme justification and validation that was brought on by the success of this war on banishing evil and restoring hope.

Complex Conflicts in the Modern Era

In contrast, the following three military operations (i.e., in Somalia, Kosovo and Rwanda) were not declared wars and did not receive a great deal of public support. Part of the lack of public support, may have been because the objectives of these operations were not entirely clear to the general public nor well defined for many of the troops who participated in them. It may have also been the case that these operations took place in distant countries that were largely unfamiliar to the general civilian population. We will examine these in greater detail in order to illustrate the many concepts relating to military mission and the notion of "just wars" that have been delineated thus far.

The Military Operation in Somalia

Operation Restore Hope

Somalia is an East African nation slightly smaller than Texas bordered by Ethiopia and Kenya on the west, by the Indian Ocean on the east and by the Gulf of Aden to the north. It also shares a small border with Djibouti to the northwest (Central Intelligence Agency, 2004). The climate is principally desert with irregular rainfall and monsoons. The Somali Republic was formed in 1960 from a merger of British Somaliland and Italian Somaliland. During the 1970's Somalia was aligned with the Soviet Union in response to the large-scale American support of Somalia's historic rival, Ethiopia (Zunes, 2002). When a military coup changed Ethiopia into a Marxist state in 1975, the U.S. and the Soviet Union switched their allegiances, with the Soviets backing the Ethiopian government and the Americans backing the Barre regime in Somalia.

From the late 1970's until Barre's overthrow in 1991, the U.S. sent hundreds of millions of dollars in arms to Somalia in exchange for the use of military facilities that had been originally constructed by the Soviet Union (Zunes, 2002). The U.S.

wanted these bases in Somalia to stage military operations in the Middle East. During the years when the Barre regime received U.S. support, thousands of civilians were massacred and civil war erupted. However, once the Cold War ended and the U.S. was allowed to establish military bases in the Persian Gulf itself, Somalia lost its strategic importance. In November 1992, the Bush administration sent 30,000 troops, primarily Marines and Rangers, to Somalia in what was described as a humanitarian mission to assist in the distribution of relief supplies for the famine stricken nation.

The mission of the forces was to secure an airfield and key installations and provide security for safe passage of relief supplies (Stewart, 2004). The UN endorsed this initiative and many Somalis, but not all, were grateful for the U.S. intervention.

Large numbers of Somalis saw the U.S. presence as representative of the former dictatorship that the U.S. had supported (Zunes, 2002). Further, since Rangers and Marines were not trained for "humanitarian" missions, skepticism and resentment towards the Americans increased among the Somalis.

At one point the purpose of the U.S. presence shifted from food distribution to disarming warlords. This resulted in armed confrontations often in crowded urban neighborhoods and increasing casualties among Somalis and American servicemen. The Somali militiamen were well armed with American weapons that had been supplied to the former dictator and the militia used these weapons aggressively to attack U.S. forces. In 1993 the U.S. attempted to have the UN take over the mission, but still wound up leading the UN forces. The conflict intensified and the mission of the U.S. troops now evolved to capturing the warlord Mohammed Aideed. A failed attempt to capture Aideed developed into a major battle in Mogadishu portrayed in the movie, "Black Hawk Down," in which 18 American Rangers were killed and more than 70 were wounded. At least 500 Somalis were killed and more than 1,000 were wounded (Reeve, 2001). Faced with increasing dissent in the U.S., past President Bill Clinton withdrew American forces in 1994. In March 1995, under Operation United Shield, the U.S. military assisted in the final withdrawal of all UN peacekeeping troops from Somalia.

The U.S. intervention in Somalia is widely considered to have been a fiasco (Zunes, 2002). None of the various missions seem to have been accomplished. This makes Somalia another "Vietnam" and a topic that is not easily broached in political arenas.

The failure of the Somalia intervention was largely responsible for the subsequent hesitation of the U.S. to engage in humanitarian interventions to prevent the genocide that was taking place in Rwanda in 1994 (Zunes). Unfortunately, Somalia cannot be so easily dismissed by the men and women who served there. There are hundreds of combat veterans who fought in this conflict and most of them were probably under the assumption that they were being deployed to provide humanitarian services and restore order to a severely distressed nation. Accordingly, the resentment and hostility they received from the Somalis must have been at the very least confusing and certainly disheartening. Very few of the U.S. troops would have predicted that they would be involved in armed combat with thousands of angry, well- armed Somali militiamen.

Being ordered to withdraw without completing the mission is not an honorable conclusion to a military operation for service members. This action generated intense feelings of anger, shame and betrayal among many Vietnam-Era veterans as it brought them back to their own experiences in Vietnam. Some veterans of the struggle in Somalia also harbor these same feelings. Although no U.S. military operation is taking place in Somalia at this time, Somalia has been identified as a base of operations for Osama bin Laden's al Qaeda and other terrorist groups (Reeve, 2001). Accordingly, there is the possibility of another special operation in Somalia.

Homecoming

There was no organized homecoming celebration for the troops that served in Somalia. There was no clear- cut victory and not even a restoration of order in Somalia. Neither the troops nor the civilians were pleased with the outcome of this operation. It is not clear at this point whether the service members have been honored for their service. It is very important that the veterans who served in Somalia have an opportunity to express their feelings about their experiences in this conflict. It may be especially important for veterans of color, particularly African Americans, to process their experiences due to the fact that they were facing an enemy who looked very much like them. They may have issues related to identification with the enemy not shared by their Caucasian comrades.

The Military Operation in Kosovo

Operation Noble Anvil

Kosovo is a province of Serbia in the core of the former Yugoslavia. It is largely occupied by ethnic Albanians, most of whom are Muslim. In 1989 President Slobodan Milosevic revoked the autonomy that had been granted to the province through the Yugoslavian constitution. The Muslim majority of Kosovo responded by forming the Kosovo Liberation Army (KLA) to not only restore their rights but to also press for full independence from Yugoslavia. Croatia, Slovenia, and Bosnia-Herzegovina all declared independence from Yugoslavia, thus, triggering ethnic fighting between Croats, Muslims, and Serbians. Serbian forces massacred thousands of Bosnian Muslims and expelled remaining Muslims and other non-Serbians from areas under Bosnian Serb control (CNN Timeline, 2004). Serbian forces then moved to eliminate the KLA and institute "ethnic cleansing" in Kosovo. This resulted in hundreds of thousands of ethnic-Albanian Muslims being driven from their homes creating a catastrophic refugee problem and a humanitarian crisis (Time Daily, 2004). Massive civilian casualties and the mounting refugee crisis prompted NATO countries to threaten military intervention if Milosevic did not cease his actions. Although Milosevic agreed to a cease-fire in late 1998, he resumed his campaign in early 1999. NATO forces subsequently began air strikes against Serbian military targets in the former Yugoslavia under Operation Allied Force. The American component of this NATO action was Operation Noble Anvil (Global Security, 2004). The mission of U.S. forces was to promote regional stability, cooperation and security in support of the international community. The goal of the U.S. and its NATO allies was to force the KLA and Milosevic to accept a compromise of restoring Kosovo's autonomy within the former Yugoslavia (Time Daily, 2004). The air strikes continued for several months, but by June 1999, Milosevic finally accepted peace terms. By that time the International Criminal Tribunal in The Hague had also indicted him for war crimes. NATO forces, including U.S. troops, were then deployed into Kosovo.

Homecoming

Although some American service members have completed their tours of duty in Kosovo, a sizable American presence is still there serving as peacekeepers. Their mission has not been completed and there seems to be no timetable for their departure. Although this may at first seem unusual, a review of U.S. military history shows that long deployments are not unusual. The U.S. stayed continuously in Haiti from 1915 to 1933 (19 years); in Nicaragua from 1910 to 1933 (23 years); in the Philippines from 1899-1946 (47 years); in China from the 1840s to the 1940s (100 years); American troops still remain in South Korea today (Boot, 2002).

Kosovo no longer receives any U.S. media attention, and the conditions there have been essentially forgotten. Unfortunately, this means that the service members who return will probably not receive any organized displays of appreciation from their respective civilian communities. For most of them, the service they provided will go unrecognized.

The Military Operation in Rwanda

Operation Quiet Resolve/Restore Hope

Rwanda is a landlocked country in central Africa that is slightly smaller than the state of Maryland. It is bordered by Tanzania on the east, the Democratic Republic of the Congo on the west, Uganda on the north and Burundi on the south. The climate is temperate with two rainy seasons and with possible frost and snow in the mountains (Central Intelligence Agency, 2004). Most of the country is savanna grassland and the population is primarily rural. In 1959, while Rwanda was still a Belgian colony, the Hutus, the largest ethnic group, overthrew the ruling Tutsi king. Over the next few years, thousands of other Tutsis were killed and over 150,000 more driven into exile in neighboring countries. In 1973, Juvenal Habyarimana, a Hutu, seized power in a coup and continued as president for the next 21 years.

The children of these exiles formed a rebel group called the Rwandan Patriotic Front (RPF). They invaded Rwanda from bases in Uganda and started a civil war in 1990. The war inflamed ethnic tensions. President Habyarimana and Burundian President Cyprian Ntaryamira were both killed in a plane crash in early 1994 and the RPF was immediately accused of assassinating President Habyarimana. This resulted in the organized campaign of violence against Tutsis during which they were referred to as "cockroaches" and "the enemy." Rwandan radio broadcasters called upon every Hutu to kill as many Tutsi as possible (U.S. Institute of Peace, 1995).

Two civilian militias trained by the Rwandan Army and affiliated with President Habyarimana were largely responsible for carrying out the genocide. They were: the Interahamwe ("Those Who Attack Together") and the Impuzamugambi ("Those Who Have the Same Goal"). Hutu soldiers, the presidential guard and the militias began to systematically hunt down and kill Tutsi civilians (U.S. Institute of Peace, 1995). In less than four months nearly 800,000 Tutsis and moderate Hutus were killed. The Tutsi Rwandan Patriotic Front defeated the Hutu regime and approximately 2,000,000 Hutus fled to neighboring countries fearing Tutsi retribution. This created a massive refugee crisis.

As horrible as the genocide had been in Rwanda, the U.S. did not intervene. Its interests had not been affected enough to launch a unilateral intervention (Ferroggiaro, 2004). Further, the U.S. did not encourage a UN response because it wanted to avoid the authorization of a new UN force and a new mandate without the means to implement either, and the Clinton Administration wanted to avoid having to retreat from another failed UN mission such as the one that had just occurred in Somalia (Ferroggiaro).

However, due to the intense publicity and media coverage that the genocide, the refugee crisis, and the subsequent famine had attained, President Clinton was forced to take action. He authorized Operation Restore Hope to aid Rwandan refugees, and deployed military personnel in Zaire, Rwanda, and Uganda. The mission of the troops was to set up the infrastructure that would support the humanitarian response. A contingent of 2,500 troops was deployed to the region and this eventually resulted in a decline of loss of life due to the famine (Wheeler, 1996). In early 1995 the U.S. began to send military advisors to the Rwandan Army. Their mission was to stabilize the military (Duke, 1997). Although Rwanda has no direct strategic values to the U.S. its stability would prevent further instability in Central Africa and it could also serve as a U.S. "zone of influence" in East Africa (Duke, 1997).

Homecoming

The homecoming for the troops who served in Operation Restore Hope was quiet. This was a humanitarian mission and the mission was successfully completed. Although there may have been no public recognition for their service, the service members themselves had the satisfaction of knowing they had helped a nation in distress and had successfully completed their mission.

The War in Afghanistan

Operation Enduring Freedom

Subsequent to the terrorists' attacks on the Pentagon and the World Trade Center, the US military began to deploy troops to South Asia. Over 30,000 active duty men and women as well as approximately 50,000 reservists were deployed to Afghanistan, Pakistan, and several neighboring former Soviet Republics (Environmental Agents Service, 2002a). The first US troops to operate in Afghanistan were Special Forces units, and conventional ground troops did not move into Afghanistan until November 2001(Environmental Agents Service, 2002b). As of January 2002, only about 4,000 of the 30,000 active duty personnel were actually in Afghanistan, the remainder of this group along with the reserve personnel were dispersed in neighboring areas, at sea, in Kuwait, and on the Island of Diego Garcia (Environmental Agents Service, 2002b). In October 2006 NATO forces took over control of U.S. forces in Afghanistan.

Risks during deployment

In addition to the risks associated with combat, the troops in this current deployment are at risk of exposure to a variety of environmental hazards (both natural and locally created), infectious diseases, and deployment –related stressors. Natural environmental health hazards include short-term health effects from exposure to sand, wind, and dust which may, in turn, cause temporary respiratory problems such as excessive coughing and nosebleeds. Another natural environmental factor that could negatively impact the health of U.S. troops is the high mountainous terrains of Afghanistan and Pakistan. Troops will be at great risk for both cold injury and "mountain illness." Cold injury could occur faster than military personnel would ordinarily expect due to the reduced oxygen and lower air pressure in the mountains. Mountain illness, which includes symptoms such as headache, nausea, vomiting, dizziness, and fatigue, occurs when individuals work at high altitudes without proper acclimatization. Unfortunately, the rapid deployment of U.S. troops, of course, leaves little time for acclimatization. The local environmental health hazards include exposure to sewage, agricultural and industrial contamination, and localized air pollution.

Although U.S. troops are protected from exposure to infectious disease through a variety of vaccinations, and have been routinely directed not to consume locally produced raw or unprocessed food products, local infectious diseases are still a concern (Environmental Agents Service, 2002a). Water contaminated with human and animal waste is considered to be widespread in Afghanistan so diseases resulting from consuming contaminated food and water such as Hepatitis A and E, cholera, and typhoid fever could be expected. Also, tuberculosis rates among Afghans are among the highest in the world (Environmental Agents Service, 2002b) and the risk of exposure to other respiratory diseases such as diphtheria and influenza is also high. Mosquito bites pose a high risk of malaria, dengue fever, and West Nile fever, while bites from sand flies could lead to leishmaniasis and sand fly fever. U.S. troops receive anti-malaria drugs and insect repellents to help to protect them against these insect-borne illnesses.

Deployment-related stressors include jet lag, change of diet, and the rapid and continuous pace of deployed military activities. Troops most at risk include those who are exposed to combat, death, or human suffering or those who are worried about home and family (Environmental Agents Service, 2002a).

Homecoming

A wide range of health problems has been anticipated in veterans returning from this deployment (Environmental Agents Service, 2002b). The majority of troops who seek health care at VA medical facilities will receive effective treatment. Some returning troops will have physical illness and some will suffer from the psychological effects of surviving the war. However, some will return with serious symptoms that will be difficult to explain (Environmental Agents Service, 2002a, 2002b).

The war in Afghanistan was initially judged a success due to the defeat of the Taliban. This swift and unexpected military victory suggests that the U.S. forces had adapted to the dynamics of the modern battlefield in order to engage unconventional opponents. On the other hand it could have meant that the Taliban were not militarily sophisticated enough to face U.S. combat troops. Fortunately, the early veterans of this conflict who defined their mission as the overthrow of the Taliban will believe they have successfully completed their mission. However, as of July 2008, U.S. forces were still at war in Afghanistan. As of September 2010, U.S. forces had experienced 1,165 deaths (952 of those killed in action), as well as 7,820 wounded in action (Department of Defense, 2010b).

The War in Iraq (2003-2010)

The Second Gulf War: Operation Iraqi Freedom

Iraq is slightly larger than twice the size of the state of Idaho. Its geography is mostly desert with a climate that is mild to cold in the winter and dry hot summers.

It was formerly part of the Ottoman Empire but became an independent kingdom in 1932. It became the Republic of Iraq in 1958. Iraq's economy is dominated by oil production. In the 1980's the financial problems caused by Iraq's eight-year war with Iran caused the Iraqi government to borrow heavily in order to finance the reconstruction of new oil pipelines and other facilities. In 1990, two years after the war with Iran ended Iraq invaded Kuwait and precipitated the First Gulf War. In 2002 U.S. troops were again deployed to the Gulf region as a result of Iraq's refusal to comply with the United Nations' mandate regarding inspections for weapons of mass destruction. U.S. troops subsequently invaded Iraq. Although coalition forces declared a decisive victory of Saddam Hussein's regime during April 2003, American troops were engaged in combat in Iraq until August 2010.

In early 2003 U.S. military strategists estimated that 200 lightly armored personnel carriers would be all that was needed for the invasion and occupation of Iraq. By May of 2004 they had changed their estimate to 20 times that number (Gibbs, 2004). In 2003 the U.S. Central Command predicted that 150,000 troops would be needed for the invasion of Iraq and that the number could be reduced by 30,000 as early as September 2005 (Gibbs). However, the loss of allied troops from Spain followed by Honduras and the Dominican Republic seemed to have caused U.S. military strategists to reconsider their timetable. During April 2003, the month that Baghdad fell, 37 American troops were killed. As of February 2004, U.S. casualties included 501 deaths, 378 of which were the result of hostile actions. Although the U.S. transferred control of the government to Iraqi citizens, American troops were still deployed in Iraq and continued to be targets of insurgents and terrorists through July 2008. As of August 2006, 2,591 U.S. service members had been killed (2,055 killed in action) and 10,547 were wounded (8,840 not returned to duty) (Department of Defense, 2006). As of September 2010, 4,408 U.S. service members had been killed (3,483 killed in action), and 31,929 were wounded (Department of Defense, 2010b).

Homecoming

On August 31, 2010, President Barrack Obama declared Operation Iraqi Freedom over. At this time all of the nearly 100,000 combat troops were pulled out of the country; however 50,000 troops have remained as advisors. This transitional group of troops will have the mission of advising and assisting Iraq's Security Forces, supporting Iraqi troops in targeted counter-terrorism missions, and protecting civilians. These troops are scheduled to leave Iraq by the end of 2011 (Fox News, 2010; Kornblut, 2010).

It is expected that the homecoming for these veterans will mirror the experiences of the veterans from Afghanistan. The majority of service members will return in good health. However, some will have physical illness and physical injuries, and some will suffer from the psychological effects of surviving the war. Some may also return with serious symptoms that will be difficult to explain. The Armed Forces Surveillance Center reported 178,876 total service members with Traumatic Brain Injury since 2000 (Defense and Veterans Brain Injury Center, 2010). A study conducted by the RAND Corporation found that nearly 20% of Iraq and Afghanistan veterans report symptoms of Post Traumatic Stress Disorder or major depression. Of these service members, just more than half actually seek care for their symptoms (Center for Military Health Policy Research, 2008).

World War IV (2001-present)

The Global War on Terrorism

World Word IV is a term first used by Dr. Eliot Cohen of the John Hopkins School for Advancement of International Studies in a November, 2001 Wall Street Journal editorial to describe the global warfare in which the United States is currently engaged. The former U.S. national security doctrine focused on containment of the spread of Soviet-style communism, nuclear deterrence, and balance of power. This doctrine was used effectively against the Soviet Union until its collapse in 1991. However, the demise of the former Soviet Union at the end of the Cold War (World War III) did not leave the U.S. free of enemies, and this became increasingly clear after the terrorist attacks of September 11, 2001.

The terrorist attacks also made it clear that the former national security policy, which focused on deterrence, containment, and balance of power between nations, would not be effective because terrorists have no nation or citizens to defend, no central location to protect, and no single source of weapons. Further, terrorists do not have standing armies and uniforms nor do they engage in conventional warfare since their preference is for guerilla tactics or asymmetric warfare. Asymmetric warfare refers to attempts to undermine opponents' strengths and minimize their advantages by using methods that are significantly different from the opponents' preferred methods of operation (Megis, 2003). Megis also notes that the U.S. military's overdependence on technologically intensive systems within a conventional forces framework has made it particularly vulnerable to asymmetric warfare and idiosyncratic attacks.

The Bush Doctrine, the name by which the new policy is often called, focuses on (a) identifying nations that harbor or sponsor terrorist groups, (b) preventing them from spreading weapons of mass destruction to other nations or to terrorist groups, and (c) ultimately eliminating such weapons from their arsenals. This policy now emphasizes preemptive intervention rather than defense and is based on determining potential threats to national security and then neutralizing them before they fully emerge. This means that the Global War on Terrorism requires a strategy that not only attempts to identify the enemy's evolving capabilities before they emerge but also identifies the weaknesses within one's own military organizations and civilian social structures relative to the operating structures of a potential enemy (Megis, 2003). Hence, as the Bush Doctrine suggests, the operating strategy for World War IV, of necessity, should be anticipatory and preemptive in order to be effective.

In 2001, the U.S. State Department identified seven countries as "rogue states" or sponsors of international terrorism. These countries were: Cuba, Iran, Iraq, Libya, North Korea, Sudan and Syria. Since all of these countries were seen as potential enemies of the U.S., any of them could have become the targets of U.S. special operations at some point in the future, and Iraq did, in fact, become a target.

One point of contention with this doctrine is that it essentially authorizes the U.S. military to intervene in other nations prior to any act of aggression being carried out against the U.S. This seemingly violates the sovereignty of other nations since no act of aggression has actually occurred. Also, the way in which the "enemies of the State" are determined is not altogether clear, and the opportunities for errors in intelligence seem to be great (as was the case with Iraq). Further, the members of the enemies list are subject to change quickly. For example, as of July 2008, North Korea had been removed from the list of "rogue states."

Although The Bush Doctrine is a new doctrine of national defense, one aspect of the old doctrine and the new doctrine remains the same: the further expansion of democracy throughout the world. During the Cold War (World War III), communism was the enemy of freedom and democracy, and revolutionary movements were the methods of change employed by the enemy. During World War IV, militant Islamic fundamentalism has now been named the new enemy of freedom and democracy, and terrorism has become the method of change used by the enemy (Cohen, 2001). Although the spread of democracy (and capitalism) may be to the long-term advantage of the U.S., this process may be viewed as cultural imperialism rather than modernization by many nations. Consequently, the continued spread of democracy and other American values may actually increase hostility toward the U.S., and the size of the U.S. military, particularly the ground forces of the Army and the Marines, will need to increase substantially to address both terrorism and the operational strategies proposed to combat it.

Conclusions

None of these military operations are as well known to most Americans as World War II or the Vietnam War even though they all occurred much more recently. None of them seem to have gained place in the collective consciousness of the American public and none seem to have spawned heroes, tales of valor, or patriotic zeal. In recent years OEF/OIF has become as widely known as these earlier conflicts.

In general, they seem to have been not talked about, but ironically, these are the types of military operations that are most likely to occur. Several common factors characterize these military operations. First they were U.S. interventions between competing factions within the same country and thereby seem to contradict the principle of noninterference. The conflict in Kosovo was a clear example of intervention by NATO into the internal affairs of Serbia since Kosovo was an integral part of Serbia. Very little of the national interest of the major NATO powers was involved in Kosovo so humanitarian and human rights interests were cited to override Serbian sovereignty (Cook, 2004, p.35). However, in the case of Rwanda, humanitarian concerns were not invoked. Hence the harmonization of state sovereignty with issues of human rights and humanitarian intervention remains an unresolved issue (Cook, 2004). Second, there was overt political (foreign policy) determination of military objectives that sometimes conflicted with the preferences of military leaders.

Third, each mission involved "mission creep" or a shifting peacekeeping mission for U.S. troops that was not originally present. This means that once hostilities began, there was always the propensity for troops to forget the cause that warranted the original use of force and to move on to a self-protective or offensive posture achieve. This was particularly evident when the original objectives of the operation were vague or ambiguous. Finally, these operations were interventions in failed or failing states outside the historical strategic focus of the U.S. This final characteristic is particularly important because failed or failing states have now become a permanent part of the strategic priority of the U.S. This was a lesson first learned at the end of World War I when it became apparent to U.S. military strategists that instability and power imbalance in Europe could threaten the security of the United States.

The most devastating foreign attack on the U.S. mainland in U.S. history was planned and directed by al Qaeda, an international terrorist group headquartered in a failed state, Afghanistan, under the control of the Taliban (Record, 2002). The Taliban provided safe-haven for Osama bin Laden who in return provided financial and technical assistance to the Taliban.

This type of reciprocal relationship is not unusual in failed states because weak states are often sympathetic to or at least easily influenced by terrorist organizations (Record). Thus, weak states, not strong ones have become the primary source of international instability (Record) and the major threat to U.S. security.

The global war on terrorism and other strategic endeavors require the U.S. to intervene more frequently in failed and failing nations. The military will need more practical capability in nation building and stability and support operations to achieve its strategic aims (Echevarria, 2004, p.18).

Implications for Counselors

The importance of this discussion for counselors is twofold. First, the likelihood that these types of conflicts will continue is very high, and there will be increasing numbers of veterans of these conflicts. In fact, the majority of future combat veterans will have served in this type of military operation. Second many of the enlisted personnel who participate in these operations may be conflicted about their service in these operations, especially since there is often not a great deal of public support or appreciation for their service. Veterans may feel that what they did was necessary at the time, but they may also feel that their mission was not completed because they did not do what they expected they would do.

All of these operations involved a great deal of suffering among the civilian population and especially among children. Future special operations will probably also have these characteristics because of the nature of the conflict and combatants. Many veterans probably will have seen images that they would rather have forgotten. Some of what they saw may still haunt them. More importantly for the veterans, however, will be their belief that they completed their missions in an honorable manner. Much of the counselor's task may ultimately involve helping veterans achieve this end.

Where do the current military operations in the Middle East fit into U.S. foreign policy?

This is a very good question especially since the largest population of combat veterans you may see may be from this era. As in other sections of this text it might prove most useful to begin this section with a self-assessment of terms and issues.

The current U.S. military operations in the Middle East include the operations in Afghanistan and Iran. Both operations have required a massive contingent of U.S. ground forces, and neither of the operations seems to have accomplished its initial objectives. As public opposition to the prolonged presence of U. S. forces in the Middle East continues, it will be harder for the U.S. to maintain a military presence in these areas.

Military Issues Self-Assessment
Military Precepts and Organization

Match the letter of the military precept with the words or statements that follow them.

    A. Chain of Command
    B. The Geneva Conventions
    C. Just War Doctrine
    D. Rules of Engagement
    E. Unified Code of Military Justice

1.   International agreements about how warfare should be conducted   _____

2.   Asserts that expected cost of war should not exceed costs in terms of human life and destruction of property   _____

3.   Asserts when and under what conditions soldiers return enemy fire   _____

4.   Asserts the death penalty for running away, throwing away arms and ammunition, or otherwise displaying cowardly conduct in the presence of the enemy   _____

5.   Prohibits intentionally killing women and children   _____

6.   Prohibits intentional destruction of medical facilities and equipment   _____

7.   Determine who reports to whom in a military organization   _____

8.   Requires medical treatment of the enemy sick and wounded   _____

9.   Requires regular access to communication with relatives   _____

10.   Insures clear communication of military objectives on the field   _____

11.   Determines who may serve on a court-martial   _____

12.   Asserts the death penalty for willful disobedience of a lawful command of a commissioned officer during a time of war   _____

13.   Prohibits wars based solely on revenge   _____

14. Asserts the right of service members to protect themselves during hostile encounter

_____

15. Determines the nature of relationships with civilians in the war zone.

_____

16. Asserts the legitimacy of force of arms when diplomacy fails

_____

17. Prohibits plunder and pillage of civilian or non-combatant dwellings

_____

18. Describes the organizational structure of the service branch

_____

19. Determines the line of authority and responsibility along which orders are passed

_____

20. Prohibits sexual relations between members of the same sex

_____

Match the letter of the unit of organization with the words or statements that follow
   A. Squad (crew, section)
   B. Brigade
   C. Company
   D. Division
   E. Platoon
   F. Battalion
   G. Fire team

21. A group of 62 to 250 soldiers commanded by captain

_____

22. A group of 8 to 16 soldiers led by a corporal or NCO

_____

23. A group of 16 to 44 soldiers led by a lieutenant and an NCO

_____

24. A group of 300 to 1000 soldiers let by a colonel

_____

25. A group of 2,000 to 5,000 solders let ay a colonel

_____

26. The largest military organizational unit listed

_____

27. The smallest military organizational unit listed

_____

Answers to the self-assessment (Questions 1-27):

1. B	6. B	11. E	16. C	21. C	26. D
2. C	7. A	12. E	17. E/B	22. A	27. G
3. D	8. B	13. C	18. A	23. E	
4. E	9. B	14. D	19. A	24. F	
5. B/E	10. A	15. D	20. E	25. B	

Middle Eastern /Asian Foreign Policy
Self-Assessment

This inventory is designed to assess your knowledge of basic issues and topics related to U.S. foreign policy in the Middle East. For each statement, please circle the letter of the response that best completes the statement.

1. Baghdad is the capital city of

    a. Iran
    b. Iraq
    c. Syria
    d. Damascus

2. Mesopotamia was the ancient name for

    a. Syria
    b. Iran
    c. Iraq
    d. Egypt

3. Which of the following Middle Eastern countries is known definitely to have weapons of mass destruction (WMD)?

    a. Egypt
    b. Syria
    c. Iran
    d. Iraq
    e. Israel

4. Which of the following is true about Kurdistan?

    a. It is the homeland of the Kurds
    b. It is located in northern Iraq
    c. Its population was attached by sarin and mustard gases in 1988 by order of Sadam Hussein.
    d. The population is a non-Arab ethnic group
    e. All of the above

5. Which of the following is true about Palestine?

    a. It was divided into Jordan in 1921 and Israel 1n 1948
    b. Its two main divisions are the West Bank and the Gaza Strip
    c. It has no standing army
    d. It is not a country
    e. All of the above

6.   Which of the following is not true about Israel?

      a.   Modern Israel was created by the U.S.
      b.   It receives approximately $3 billion annually from the U.S. to purchase arms and other military equipment
      c.   The Golan Heights is its primary source of water
      d.   Women are drafted to serve in the military
      e.   Muslims and Christians may volunteer for military service

7.   Which of the following issues are involved in every Middle Eastern peace accord involving Israel?

      a.   The status of Jerusalem which both Israel and Palestine claim as capitals
      b.   Israeli settlements in the West Bank and the Gaza Strip
      c.   The return of Palestinians displaced since 1948
      d.   The creation of a Palestinian state
      e.   All of the above

8.   Which of the following statements are true about the Mujahideen?

      a.   They are essentially a multinational army of militant Muslims
      b.   They have been involved in violent conflicts in Chechnya, Pakistan, and the Philippines
      c.   They were originally organized and armed by the U.S., Saudi Arabia, and Pakistan to battle the Soviets in Afghanistan in the 1980s
      d.   All of the above
      e.   None of the above

9.   Which county has the largest Muslim population?

      a.   Indonesia
      b.   Turkey
      c.   Pakistan
      d.   Saudi Arabia
      e.   India

Match the letter of the following to the words and phrases that will follow.

      i.   Afghanistan
      ii.   Pakistan
      iii. Iraq
      iv.   India
      v.   Iran

10. Founded in 1747 through unification of the Pashtun tribes   _____

11. World's largest producer of opium poppies   _____

12. Islamabad is the capital city   _____

13. Kabul fell to the Taliban in 1996   _____

14. Separated from India in 1947   _____

15. Borders Bangladesh on the East and West   _____

16. Occupied by the Soviet Union between 1979 and 1989   _____

17. Asif Zardari became president after President Musharraf resigned   _____

18. Second southwest Asian nuclear power after Pakistan   _____

19. Site of Gulf War I and Gulf War II   _____

20. Non-Arab Muslim state   _____

Military Self-Assessment
Middle Eastern Issues

Write in the letter of the statements on the following page that best match the terms listed below.

1.	Arafat, Yasser	_____	15.	Jihad	_____
2.	Al Qaeda	_____	16.	Mecca	_____
3.	Anatolia	_____	17.	Mesopotamia	_____
4.	Axis of Evil	_____	18.	Mossad	_____
5.	Ayatollah	_____	19.	Mujahideen	_____
6.	Burka	_____	20.	Persia	_____
7.	Camp David Accords	_____	21.	Rogue States	_____
8.	Desert Storm	_____	22.	Islamabad	_____
9.	Fedayeen	_____	23.	Shiites	_____
10.	Gaza Strip	_____	24.	Sunni	_____
11.	Golan Heights	_____	25.	West Bank	_____
12.	Hamas	_____	26.	Hamid Karzai	_____
13.	Hezbolla	_____			
14.	ntifada	_____			

Select the letters from among the following statements that match the terms on the proceeding page:

a.   Very small section of southern Palestine bordered by the Mediterranean Sea and Egypt and almost completely fenced in by Israel

b.   Anti-Israeli Islamic resistance movement based in Palestine

c.   Arabic term for "struggles" currently used to mean "holy war"

d.   Former Chairman of the PLO

e.   Ancient name for the area that is now Turkey

f.   Title given to scholars of Islamic law

g.   Name for the 1991 Persian Gulf War

h.   Southwest corner of Syria currently occupied by Israel

i.   Lebanese anti-Israeli resistance group backed by Iran

j.   Arabic term for " uprising" typically referring to Palestinian insurrections against Israel

k.   Northern section of Palestine bordered by Jordan to the East and nearly completely fenced in by Israel.

l   City in southwestern Saudi Arabia where the Prophet Muhammad was born in 570 A.D.

m.   Former name for Iran

n.   Current capital of Pakistan

o.   Larger branch of Islam to which 90% of Muslims belong.

p.   Peace agreement brokered by President Jimmy Carter in which Israel agreed to return the Sinai region to Egypt and Egypt agreed to recognize Israel's right to exist.

q   President G.W. Bush's name for North Korea, Iran and Iraq

r.   Militant Islamic organization responsible for the 9/11 attacks in New York and Washington, D.C.

s.   Veil that covers the entire body of a woman including her face with the exception of a patch of netting that covers her eyes

t.   First democratically elected president of Afghanistan

u.   Arabic word for "guerilla fighters"; particularly those who are anti-Israeli

v.   Ancient name for Iraq

w.   Israeli secret service that assassinates enemies of Israel

x.   Arabic word meaning "holy warrior"

y.   Countries that the U.S, government believes sponsor terrorism

z.   Branch of Islam believing religious leaders should only be descendants of the Prophet Muhammad.

Answers: Middle Eastern/ Asian Foreign Policy Assessment

1. b	6. a	13. a	18. d
2 c	7. e	14 b	19. c
3. e	8. a	15 d	20. e
4. e	9. a	16. a	
5. e	10. a	17. b	

Answers: Middle Eastern Issues

1. d	9.u	16.s	23. z
2.r	10.a	17. m	24. o
3.e	11.h	18. w	25. k
4.q	12. b	19. x	26. t
5.f	13. i	20. v	
7.p	14. j	21. y	
8.g	15. c	22. N	

Chapter 3

Counseling and Services in the Military

What is the VA and what is its role in helping veterans?

The "VA" is a term used by military service members and civilians to refer to either the Department of Veterans Affairs, or to a Veterans Administration Hospital or to the Veterans Administration. The Veterans Administration was created in 1930 by Executive Order 5398 signed by President Herbert Hoover (Woolley & Peters, 2010). In 1989 the "VA" became the Department of Veterans Affairs. The VA is now the second largest of the 15 Cabinet departments and operates programs for health care, financial assistance and other federal benefits to veterans and their families throughout the nation (Department of Veterans Affairs, 2009a).

As of April 2010, the VA had 300,640 employees (National Center for Veterans Analysis and Statistics, 2010). Only the Department of Defense has a larger work force. The majority (210, 432) was in the Veterans Health Administration, and the second largest group (12,962) was employed in the Veterans Benefits Administration. The VA's fiscal year 2010 projected spending is $112.8 billion -- $47.4 for health care, $56.923 billion for benefits, and $242 million for the national cemetery system (Department of Veterans Affairs, 2009a). President Obama is seeking $125 billion for the VA's fiscal year 2011 budget (Department of Veterans Affairs, 2010e).

Medical Care

Perhaps the most visible of all VA benefits and services is health care. From 54 hospitals in 1930, VA's health care system has grown to 153 hospitals (National Center for Veterans Analysis and Statistics, 2010), with at least one in each state, Puerto Rico and the District of Columbia. VA operates 909 ambulatory care and community-based outpatient clinics, 135 nursing homes, 47 residential rehabilitation treatment programs and 108 comprehensive home-care programs. VA health care facilities provide a broad spectrum of medical, surgical and rehabilitative care. Almost 5.5 million people received care in VA health care facilities in 2008. By the end of fiscal year 2008, 78 percent of all disabled and low-income veterans had enrolled with VA for health care; 65 percent of them were treated by the VA (Department of Veterans Affairs, 2009a).

In 2008, VA inpatient facilities treated 773,600 patients. VA's outpatient clinics registered nearly 60 million visits (Department of Veterans Affairs, 2009a). The VA manages the largest medical education and health professions training program in the United States. Veterans Affairs facilities are affiliated with 107 medical schools, 55 dental schools and more than 1,200 other schools across the country. Each year, about 90,000 health professionals are trained in VA medical centers. More than half of the physicians practicing in the United States had some of their professional education in the VA health care system (Department of Veterans Affairs, 2009a). Since 1996, the VA has put its health care facilities under 21 networks that provide more medical services to more veterans and family members than at any time during the VA's long history (Department of Veterans Affairs, 2009a).

Eligibility for Services

Veterans must enroll to receive VA health care benefits. After applying for enrollment a veteran's eligibility will be verified. Veterans with a service-connected disability of 50 percent or more disabling and veterans determined by the VA to be unemployable due to service-connected conditions are given first priority. Next priority is given to veterans with lower percentages of service-connected disabilities, former POWs, Purple Heart recipients, those with a disability that began in the line of duty, and those who are disabled because of VA treatment or participation in VA vocational rehabilitation programs. Lowest priority is given to those veterans who have previously been denied enrollment in the VA health care system because their income exceeded VA's income thresholds (Military, 2010b).

As of April 2010, 8.061 million veterans were enrolled in the VA health care system (National Center for Veterans Analysis and Statistics, 2010). When veterans enroll, they are placed in priority groups or categories that help the VA manage health care services within budgetary constraints and ensure quality of care for those enrolled. Disability compensation is the monthly benefit veterans receive who were disabled by injury or disease incurred during active military service. Veterans with low incomes and who are permanently and totally disabled also may be eligible for support through VA's pension program. In fiscal year 2008, VA provided $38.9 billion in disability compensation, death compensation and pension to 3.7 million people (Department of Veterans Affairs, 2009a). About 3.1 million veterans received disability compensation or pensions from VA (National Center for Veterans Analysis and Statistics, 2010). Also receiving VA benefits were 554,700 spouses, children and parents of deceased veterans. Among them, 170,144 are survivors of Vietnam-era veterans and 235,000 are survivors of World War II (Department of Veterans Affairs, 2009a).

Homeless Veterans

The VA provides health care and benefits to more than 100,000 homeless veterans each year. While the proportion of veterans among the homeless is declining, VA actively engages veterans in outreach, medical care, benefits assistance and transitional housing.

The VA has made more than 450 grants for transitional housing, service centers and vans for outreach and transportation to state and local governments, tribal governments, non-profit community and faith-based service providers. Programs for alcoholism, drug addiction and post-traumatic stress disorder have been expanded in recent years, along with attention to environmental hazards (Department of Veterans Affairs, 2009a).

Education and Training

The Post 9/11 GI Bill became effective for training on or after August 1, 2009, and provides financial support for education and housing to individuals with at least 90 days of aggregate service on or after September 11, 2001, or individuals discharged with a service-connected disability after 30 days. In order to be eligible an individual must have received an honorable discharge. The amount of support that an individual may qualify depends on where they live and what type of degree they are pursuing. In some instances service members are able to transfer their GI Bill to dependants (Department of Veterans Affairs, 2010f).

The Post 9/11 GI Bill will pay tuition based upon the highest in-state tuition charged by a public educational institution in the state where the educational institution is located, whether or not the student attends a public institution. If the service member is attending a private institution, graduate school, or attending in an out-of-state status, and subsequently their tuition and fees exceed the amount funded by the Post 9/11 BI Bill, the Yellow Ribbon Program may provide additional funds without an additional charge. The Yellow Ribbon Program allows institutions of higher learning in the United States to voluntarily enter into an agreement with the VA to offer specific veteran Post 9/11 scholarships which the VA will, in return match (Department of Veterans Affairs, 2010g).

Since 1944, when the first GI Bill began more than 21.8 million veterans, service members and family members have received $83.6 billion in GI Bill benefits for education and training (Department of Veterans Affairs, 2009a). There were 7.8 million GI Bill recipients from World War II, 2.4 million from the Korean War and 8.2 million post-Korean and Vietnam era recipients. Since the dependents program was enacted in 1956, the VA also has assisted in the education of more than 784,000 dependents of veterans whose deaths or total disabilities were service-connected (Department of Veterans Affairs, 2009a).

Since the Vietnam-era, there have been approximately 2.7 million veterans, service members, reservists and National Guardsmen who have participated in the Veterans' Educational Assistance Program, established in 1977, and the Montgomery GI Bill, established in 1985 (Department of Veterans Affairs, 2009a). In 2008, VA helped pay for the education or training of 336,527 veterans and active-duty personnel, 106,092 reservists and National Guardsmen and 80,079 survivors (Department of Veterans Affairs, 2009a).

Vocational Rehabilitation

The VA's Vocational Rehabilitation and Employment Program provide services to enable veterans with service-connected disabilities to achieve maximum independence in daily living, and to obtain and maintain employment. During fiscal years 1999 through 2008, 86,983 program participants achieved rehabilitation by obtaining and maintaining suitable employment. Additionally, during that same period, 21,108 participants achieved rehabilitation through maximum independence in daily living (Department of Veterans Affairs, 2009a).

Home Loan Assistance

From 1944, when VA began helping veterans purchase homes under the original GI Bill, through January 2009, about 18.4 million VA home loan guarantees have been issued, with a total value of $967 billion. VA began fiscal year 2008 with 2.1 million active home loans reflecting amortized loans totaling $220.8 billion (Department of Veterans Affairs, 2009a). In fiscal year 2007, the VA guaranteed 179,000 loans valued at $36.1 billion. During the fiscal year 2008, VA's programs for specially adapted housing helped about 550 disabled veterans with grants totaling more than $24.6 million (Department of Veterans Affairs, 2009a).

Insurance

The VA operates one of the largest life insurance programs in the world. VA directly administers six life insurance programs. In addition, VA supervises the Service-members' Group Life Insurance and the Veterans' Group Life Insurance programs. These programs provide $1.3 trillion in insurance coverage to 4 million veterans, active-duty members, reservists and Guardsmen, plus 3.1 million for spouses and children (Department of Veterans Affairs, 2009a). In 2007, the VA life insurance programs returned $354 million in dividends to 1 million veterans holding these VA life insurance policies, and paid an additional $1.1 billion in death claims and other disbursements (Department of Veterans Affairs, 2009a).

Research

In 2011, funding for VA Medical Care and Prosthetics research will be $590 million (Office of Management and Budget, 2010), and another $403 million came from the VA's medical care account support research efforts. Funding from non-VA sources, such as the National Institutes of Health, contributed another $656 million to VA research as well as other government agencies and pharmaceutical companies. The VA also conducts an array of research on some of the most difficult challenges facing medical science today. It has become a world leader in such research areas as aging, women's health, AIDS, post-traumatic stress disorder and other mental health issues (Department of Veterans Affairs, 2009a).

Researchers at the VA have played key roles in developing innovations in medicine. VA contributions to medical knowledge have won VA scientists many awards, including the Nobel Prize (Department of Veterans Affairs, 2009a). The first liver transplant in the world was performed by a VA surgeon-researcher. Clinical trials conducted at VA medical centers established the effectiveness of new treatments for tuberculosis, schizophrenia and high blood pressure. Also, the "Seattle Foot," a specially engineered prosthesis that allows lower limb amputees to run and engage in active movements, was developed in a VA medical center (Department of Veterans Affairs, 2009a). Seventy-five percent of VA researchers are practicing physicians; because of their dual roles (physician-researcher), the VA research findings and medical innovations, will often be immediately applied to their patients, thus benefiting them. Functional electrical stimulation, a technology using controlled electrical currents to activate paralyzed muscles, is being developed at VA clinical facilities and laboratories throughout the country. Through this technology, paraplegic patients have been able to grasp objects, stand and even walk short distances. Special VA "centers of excellence" throughout the nation conduct research in rehabilitation, health services and medical conditions including AIDS, alcoholism, schizophrenia, stroke and Parkinson's disease. Multi-center clinical trials investigate the best therapy for various diseases.

Current projects include testing whether intensive control of blood sugar can reduce cardiovascular problems for patients with type 2 diabetes and comparing deep brain stimulation with other treatments for Parkinson's disease (Department of Veterans Affairs, 2009a). VA investigators continue to make major contributions to understanding PTSD Agent Orange exposure, and the possible health effects of environmental exposures among Gulf War veterans.

National Cemeteries

In 1973, the Army transferred 82 national cemeteries to the VA, which now manages them through its National Cemetery Administration. Currently, the VA maintains 131 national cemeteries in 39 states and Puerto Rico (Department of Veterans Affairs, 2010a). The VA administers the Presidential Memorial Certificate program, which provides gold embossed certificates signed by the president to commemorate honorably discharged, deceased veterans. They are sent to the veteran's next of kin and loved ones. The VA provided 511,353 certificates in 2008 (Department of Veterans Affairs, 2009a).

Finally, the VA also administers the State Cemetery Grants Program, which encourages the development of state veterans' cemeteries. The VA provides up to 100 percent of the funds to develop, expand or improve veterans' cemeteries operated and maintained by the states. More than $344 million has been awarded for 72 operational veterans cemeteries in 38 states, Saipan and Guam (Department of Veterans Affairs, 2009a).

What does "service connected disability" mean?

Disability ratings are a major concern for many veterans and their families. The two issues involved for veterans are (a) determining that a disability is service-connected, and (b) determining that the disability is rated at the appropriated level. Whether you become involved in the adjudication process or not, this is an issue with which you should be familiar. In order for a veteran to receive compensation for a disability, he or she must provide evidence that the disability is a result of or occurred during the course of him or her performing her assigned duties while on active duty. Physical disabilities are not as hard to document as other medical conditions or psychological disabilities.

Physical disabilities, such as the loss of a limb, are observable and the proximal cause of the disability, i.e., an explosion, is fairly easy to verify. On the other hand, medical conditions, e.g., Gulf War Syndrome, and particularly psychological disabilities, e.g., PTSD are not easily verified as being service connected.

For example, although the military agrees that PTSD is an acquired mental condition that may be manifested any time after an individual experiences an horrific event, and that military service may involve such events, in order to establish service connection for PTSD, a veteran must establish that she or he was exposed to a stressor that would cause the characteristic symptoms of PTSD to be presented in almost anyone.

Evidence of combat or evidence of being a prisoner of war is typically accepted as evidence of a stressor that would induce PTSD. However, evidence of combat does not mean simply being present in a combat environment; it means conclusive evidence such as being wounded and receiving the Purple Heart, receiving the Combat Infantryman

Badge, or some other similar citation. Because PTSD may have a delayed onset in veterans, many will not remember where they were when the traumatic event occurred.

Also there may be no documentation of a particular military operation to which they were assigned. Further, a military operation that is defined, as a "humanitarian operation" may not qualify as "combat exposure" even if hostile forces may have fired upon service members. In addition, medical and psychological appraisal must establish a clear diagnosis of PTSD and link the diagnosis to a stressor or stressors that occurred during activity.

At this point, VA personnel make three decisions: (a) whether the diagnosis of PTSD is valid, (b) whether the claim for service connection is valid, and (c) if the conditions for both "a" and "b" are met, what level of disability rating (0% to 100% total and permanent) does the disability merit. Accordingly, a veteran may display the symptoms of PTSD and receive a diagnosis of PTSD by the VA officials but fail to prove that the stressor or stressors that caused the PTSD were related to active duty service. The result would then be no disability rating and consequently no compensation for the disability. Alternatively, the veteran may receive the diagnosis of PTSD and service connection for the disorder but then receive a low disability rating. In this case the veteran's disability allowance might not allow him or her enough income to stop working. Either alternative is open to appeal, but of these outcomes usually result in a great deal of anger, frustration, and "VA hatred" for veterans and their families.

Mental Health Services

Veterans with service-connected disabilities receive priority access to care for hospitalization and outpatient care. Since 1979, VA's Readjustment Counseling Service has operated community centered "Vet Centers." Vet Centers provide psychological counseling for war-related trauma, community outreach and referral, case management and supportive social services to veterans and their family members. There are 232 Vet Centers throughout the U.S (National Center for Veterans Analysis and Statistics, 2010). Since the Vet Center Program was established by Congress in 1979, more than 2 million veterans have been helped. Every year, the Vet Centers serve over 130,000 veterans and provide over one million visits to veterans and family members (Department of Veterans Affairs, 2009a). Vet Centers are open to any veteran who served in the military in a combat theater during wartime or anywhere during a period of armed hostilities. Vet Centers also provide trauma counseling to veterans who were sexually assaulted or harassed while on active duty.

Who are the military's mental health professionals?

The military has a number of human services and medical personnel including psychologists, psychiatrists, nurses, social workers and chaplains, but it does not have what is often referred to as "mental health counselors." The professionals that are called "counselors" in the military are vocational and rehabilitation counselors who work primarily with veterans regarding career training and job placement after they are no longer on active duty. Psychiatrists, social workers, and psychologists are the providers for mental health services.

In general, enlisted personnel are reluctant to report any complaints that may suggest mental health related issues. There are several reasons for this disinclination. First, they wish to avoid a poor performance rating. Service members who are career military personnel are very sensitive to anything that might threaten their opportunities for promotion, advancement in rank, or longevity in the service. Secondly, they do not wish to run the risk of losing security clearance. Any signs of psychological distress could result in a service member being viewed as a potential security risk. This would have immediate and profound results in terms of occupational choice, rank, and pay. Thirdly, some of the topics that enlisted personnel or officers may wish to discuss may involve questionable military actions, foreign policy, or secret military operations and these topics, particularly during times of war, are not to be questioned or discussed.

In theory, military law does allow service members to have dissenting opinions about issues and policies, and in practice dissention is seldom viewed in favorable light. Additionally, there is no guarantee of confidentiality in discussing these matters (except theoretically--with chaplains). Fourthly, they would not want to be perceived as unfit for duty, and lose the trust of other members of their basic unit. There is still the perception in military culture that mental illness is a sign of weakness, and this attitude is shared by officers as well as enlisted personnel. A weak soldier, one who is not physically or mentally fit, jeopardizes the safety of all of the other members of the group; thus, no soldier would wish to be viewed as a liability to the group.

Although veterans who have completed their military service are more willing to seek mental health services than those on active duty, services are not always readily available. Mental health services are provided to veterans free of charge at Veterans Administration Hospitals, but there is often very long wait times for veterans to be seen. One reason for this delay in services, may be that veterans of more recent wars (i.e., post-Vietnam) are much more willing to seek mental health services than those of past wars. At this point, the VA hospitals have more clients than they can accommodate. For these reasons, civilian counselors are a safe alternative to military support staff for issues related to mental heath.

The role of chaplains in counseling service members in the military

The formal role of chaplains and enlisted religious support personnel in the military is to provide religious/spiritual support to military members, their families, and other authorized personnel. Their mission is to "nurture the living, care for the sick or wounded, minister to prisoners or prisoners of war, and honor the dead"(Military,

2010a, Chaplains section, para. 2). Although chaplains represent many different denominations, they are expected to provide spiritual support to all service members.

Chaplains are ordained by individual religious denominations before they join the military, and they cannot continue to practice without the endorsement of their respective denominations (Defense Jobs, 2004). Chaplains must have a graduate degree to include a minimum of 72 semester hours from an accredited institution; not less than 36 of these hours must be in theological/ministry and related studies (National Conference on Ministry to the Armed Forces, 2010). Chaplains also must have served in a church, synagogue, or mosque for 1 to 3 years as determined by their respective denominations. Chaplains must meet the physical fitness standards of the branch of service to which they are assigned (Roots, 2002). Upon joining the military, chaplains become commissioned officers in the Army, Navy or Air Force. Navy Chaplains serve with the Marine Corps and Coast Guard. Their primary role is to provide religious worship services, rites, sacraments, ordinances, and ministrations to military members and their families worldwide. Chaplains also assist military personnel with personal concerns such as faith issues, stress, anxiety, redeployment or reunion issues, moral and ethical conflicts, and social concerns.

Chaplains are often the first person service members are likely to discuss problems with who are outside their chain of command. One reason for this is that chaplains have privileged communication. Anything shared with a chaplain remains confidential. Chaplains cannot be legally compelled to disclose what has occurred in a privileged communication. In their role as advisors, chaplains help to resolve problems by making appropriate referrals to command channels or social service agencies. They also assist military personnel in requesting emergency leave, compassionate reassignments, and hardship discharges. If the request is based on medical problems of a family member, a signed statement from the attending physician is required. If the request is based on legal problems a licensed attorney must issue a statement. If the request is based on reasons other than medical or legal problems, supporting statements from responsible persons who have personal knowledge of the matter must be included. Final approval must be through the Army Human Resources Command (Department of the Army, 2007).

Chaplains are not required to have training in counseling or in mental health. Accordingly, they do not actually provide mental health counseling to service members. They are able to make referrals. Military chaplains may appear to be similar to civilian clergy, but their lives are very different to their civilian counterparts, because military chaplains are members of the armed forces. They experience the same stress of separation and reunion as other service members and they are also expected to share in the dangers of armed conflict when the time arises (Defense Jobs, 2004). The chaplain is also a member of the personnel support team and as such, is expected to be an advisor to commanders and staff on the spiritual welfare and morale of service members. Even though chaplains are not in the chain of command, they do serve as advisors to senior command and staff.

In the past, the dual aspects of the chaplain role have not always been well received by service members. Even though they have the right of privileged communication they also serve as advisors to senior command staff; therefore, some service members are uncertain that what they reveal may not become known to others. Also, in their role as officers, chaplains also have the responsibility of maintaining the morale of service members and this often entails encouraging them to continue with their missions even when it involves taking human life, and by reminding them, in effect, that God is on their side. Many veterans report being unsettled by this role of the chaplain.

Social Workers

Social workers working with veterans perform a variety of tasks. A major focus is the treatment of veteran's mental health issues such as depression, anxiety, and PTSD. Other roles include helping veterans to navigate through government bureaucracies and providing referrals to legal, financial, housing, and vocational resources (Merzoff, 2010). Savitsky, Illingworth, and DuLaney (2009), discuss how civilian social workers can provide services to the military and veteran population in areas such as education, child welfare, domestic violence, mental health, healthcare, substance abuse, and criminal justice. Social workers can familiarize themselves with military culture, policies, and practices, and provide referrals and psycho-education to veterans regarding military related problems. This can include the stressors that accompany multiple deployments, school transitions [for children], and combat-induced injuries. Civilian social workers should also be prepared to provide direct mental health services to service members, veterans, and their families (Savitsky et al., 2009). By recognizing and adopting a proactive approach to the challenges facing military and veteran clients, social workers can provide an important link to services to help reintegrate service members and their families into civilian life.

The Impact of Combat on Veterans & Counselors Interacting with Military Personnel

The impact of engaging in combat on service members

Combat is the principle activity that differentiates the military from other hierarchical organizations existing within American society. Combat is the ultimate objective of soldiers, the consummation of their training (Kegan & Holmes, 1985). The U.S. military is the only American organization in which its members are expected to use deadly force in order to protect American interests and to subdue and destroy enemies of the State. Although service members are keenly aware of this duty, the overwhelming majority of them have had no prior direct experience in using deadly force against a human opponent. Specifically, none of them will have had experienced using firearms to intentionally harm another human being.

Kegan and Holmes (1985) note that the sensations soldiers experience are complex and diverse ranging from paralyzing fear to serene heroism. They go on to state that the first contact with the enemy is often anticlimactic because men who have agonized over how they will perform in battle respond automatically. The first shots fired in combat may be just a reaction to military training that creates an abstract image of the enemy. For others, this experience may even be pleasurable either because of the sheer satisfaction of hitting a difficult target or because of outwitting a cunning adversary or because of hatred for an enemy whose death gratifies the desire for revenge (Kegan & Holmes, p. 267).

Consequently, actually taking the life of someone is a life-altering event for the majority of service members. Grossman (1996) states that "making an independent reasoned decision to kill another person, and watching as he [or she] dies due to [the soldier's own] actions combine to form the single most basic, primal, and potentially traumatic occurrence of war" (p. 79). This is neither a natural nor an easy act to accomplish, and it is also an act that the vast majority of civilians will never be called upon to perform.

It is also important to note that this discussion is focused on the experience of enlisted personnel for the most part and not that of officers. Officers typically (but not always) experience warfare in a different way than enlisted service members by providing the directives or mission order. Both commissioned officers and non-commissioned officers (NCOs) may suffer from the psychological consequences of committing violent acts and are weighed down by the knowledge that the lives of their subordinates hang in the balance of their decisions (Kegan & Holmes, 1985).

The combat soldier, however, appears to feel a deep sense of responsibility and accountability for what he sees around him. It is as though every dead enemy is a human being he has brought down, and every friendly dead is a comrade for whom he was responsible for (Grossman, 1996). Whatever the average soldier's preconceptions about armed combat may have been, few soldiers are adequately prepared to assimilate the dynamics of the encounter. "Not only do the psyches of average soldiers resist killing in combat [along with] the obligation to kill, but the soldiers themselves are also equally horrified by the inescapable fact that someone else hates him enough to want to kill him" (Grossman, 1996, p. 75). The notion of being hated is a novel, confusing and deeply disturbing experience for most American service members. In addition, even the soldier who grows accustomed to death in general will still be affected by the death of one of his comrades. The death of a comrade is more than just depressing because it destroys one of the props that sustain a soldier's morale. It also suggests to him that his or her own death may be near (Kegan & Holmes, 1985).

Overcoming Resistance

Prior to World War II (WW II) it had been assumed that the average soldier would fire at the enemy in combat simply because his country and his leaders had told him to do so as well as because it was his duty to defend his own life and the lives of his comrades (Grossman, 1996). However, the U.S. Army made two very important discoveries after interviewing thousands of Army troops about their combat experiences. They found that men in combat are usually motivated to fight not by ideology, hate, or fear. Instead, they are motivated by group pressure and a process involving (a) Unit cohesion or regard for their comrades, (b) chain of command or respect for their leaders, (c) concern for their own reputations and (d) the mission—urge to contribute to the success of the group (Grossman, 1996).

Second, they discovered that only 15 to 20 out of every 100 men would actually fire their weapons during an encounter with the enemy (Grossman, 1996). These results were the same whether soldiers were in the European or the Pacific theater. Only 15 to 20 percent of American soldiers in combat during WWII fired at the enemy (Grossman). These findings resulted in a number of changes in military training that resulted in a firing rate of 55 percent in Korea, and according to a study by Scott (1993) a firing rate of 90 to 95 percent in Vietnam. The essential difference in the revised training method was realism. In the old method soldiers stood in a line side-by-side and fired at bulls eye targets in the distance on the firing range. In revised training methods soldiers stood in trenches in full battle gear and fired at human shaped targets that popped up and/or moved at a variety of distances on the firing range, and when they hit the target, it would fall over. This newer training method increased the rate of fire from 15% to 90%. This is also the reason many contemporary combat veterans report "being on automatic" to describe their feelings during combat. The training is demonstrated to be very effective.

The Distance Factor

There is still a difference between expending rounds in a firefight or ambush and actually seeing another human being die directly as a result of the use of a weapon. When soldiers do abolish the enemy, they appear to go through a series of psycho-emotional stages. The act itself is usually described as being automatic or as a reflex action. Immediately following, the soldier typically experiences a period of euphoria and elation subsequently followed by a period of guilt and remorse. The intensity and duration of these periods is a function of the distance at which the encounter takes place: "the closer the distance, the more intense the reactions" (Grossman, 1996, p.111). When the soldier kills at close range, it is by its very nature an intensely vivid and personal matter. Hence, at close range, the euphoria stage, although brief, fleeting and not often mentioned, still appears to be experienced in some form by most soldiers (Grossman, 1996, p.115). At longer ranges the feelings are not as intense.

Distance in war is not merely physical. There is also emotional distance. Emotional distance permits the soldier to deny that he is taking the life of another human being (Grossman, 1996). Emotional distance occurs in three broad categories: cultural distance, moral distance, and social distance. Cultural distance refers to the degree to which the enemy is racially, ethnically, and linguistically different from oneself. The principle underpinning cultural distance is that it is much harder to relate to someone who looks distinctly different from you than someone who looks similar to you or who looks familiar to you. The greater the physical differences, the easier to commit violent acts against (Grossman). The ultimate cultural distance involves recasting the enemy as a subhuman life form. Accordingly, dehumanizing the enemy through propaganda and racial and ethnic slurs becomes a major psychological aspect of warfare.

Achieving cultural distance in modern warfare is not automatic nor is it a simple matter, and this is especially true in the U.S. military. Since WWII, the U.S. armed forces have been a multiracial/multiethnic organization with service members representing all major religions and ethnic groups. In modern military operations, U.S. troops will invariably face an enemy that is ethnically and/or racially similar.

Holm (1992) and Parson (1984) reported psychological tension and ambivalence among African American as well as Asian American Pacific Islander veterans toward fighting the Vietnamese because the dire condition of the Vietnamese was similar to their own in the United States. Clinical case studies of Asian American Pacific Islander Vietnam veterans describe psychological conflicts that arose because they personally identified with the Vietnamese as being of the same race (Loo, 1994). A survey conducted in a study by Matsuoka, Hamada, Kilauano, and Coalson (1992) revealed that Vietnam veterans of color reported emotional difficulties and psychological distress when encountering Vietnamese troops because they perceived them to be similar to themselves. Failing to achieve cultural distance increases the likelihood of psychological distress for the veteran.

Moral distance involves legitimizing oneself and one's cause. It can generally be divided into three components. The first component involves the determination and condemnation of the enemy's guilt, which of course, must be punished or avenged. The second is an affirmation of the legality and legitimacy of one's own cause. Moral distance establishes that the enemy's cause is clearly wrong, his leaders are criminal, and his soldiers are either simply misguided or are sharing in their leader's guilt. The third component involves believing that your course of action has been endorsed by god, thus not only is the enemy's case wrong; but it is also evil. The enemy soldiers are therefore either godless or agents of evil. The enemy is still human, but taking his life is an act of justice rather than the act of extermination that is often motivated by cultural distance (Grossman, 1996, p. 164). American wars have been characterized, at least outwardly, by a tendency toward moral distance rather than cultural distance (Grossman, 1996). The Just Wars Doctrine is currently the formal means the U.S. military uses to achieve moral distance as well as moral superiority. As noted previously, cultural difference is not a viable concept within the U.S. military.

Social distance (differences in social class) has essentially vanished as a form of emotional distance in Western warfare. However, it has been replaced by a new technologically-based form of psychological distance referred to as "Nintendo warfare" (Grossman, 1996, p. 169). The term Nintendo warfare is not intended to minimize the danger inherent in warfare, rather, it is used to describe the impact that night-vision devices and thermal imagery technology have had on the soldier's perception of the battlefield and of enemy combatants. Until recently night-sight was a rare technique of warfare; unavailable to the average soldier. Now the U.S. military fights primarily at night. Soldiers are equipped with night-vision goggles that essentially convert enemy troops into green human-shaped blobs. Thermal imagery devices are able to "see" the enemy by means of the heat emitted from their bodies (Grossman). This technology converts enemy combatants into red and orange blobs. The integration of night-vision devices and thermal-imagery technology in modern warfare radically changes the soldier's perception of the battlefield such that it becomes very similar to watching a video game on a television screen. Instead of seeing armed men and their weapons, the solider sees green or red and orange blobs moving in the distance. His goal is simply to destroy any blobs that appear on the screen. This type of tactical and technological advantage in modern warfare greatly increases the probability that soldiers will consistently fire at the enemy.

The downside of this technological advantage is that it does not allow the soldier to be sure he is aiming towards an enemy combatant. Since all human forms appear as green, red or orange blobs, there is no way to be sure one of those blobs was not a woman or a child. As Grossman (1996) notes, if a soldier hits a child or a woman or anyone else that is not actually a combatant, it is difficult for him to rationalize that the act was legitimate. Even in self-defense, soldiers typically find it difficult to view their actions in terms other than murder (Grossman). Accidentally (or intentionally) inflicting harm on a woman or child is perceived as an intensely shameful event for the majority of combat veterans. It may also be the precipitating event for subsequent psychological and emotional distress that the veteran may experience.

Crossing the Line

Many deaths in modern combat take place in ambushes and surprise attacks in which the enemy represents no immediate threat but is targeted anyway, without opportunity to surrender. Such an act is by no means considered an atrocity but it is also distinctly different from honorable and potentially harder for the soldier to rationalize and accommodate (Grossman, 1996).

This was particularly true for Vietnam era veterans who had grown up under the influence of Hollywood where only the "bad guys" ambushed anyone. The responses of contemporary American veterans may be similar. Paradoxically, many soldiers experience battle as a "half remembered blur" (Kegan & Holmes, 1985. p. 263). For some the memory of war is one of relived horror and suffering, but for the majority, war is recalled in "tones of light and shade with the warmth of comradeship and the pride of achievement and shared endeavor set alongside the anguish of anticipation and the shock of battle and the misery of privation" (Kegan & Holmes, p. 259).

National Guard and Reservists Issues

Lastly, it is critical that we discuss briefly the utilization of the National Guard and Reservist within the current conflicts in Iraq and Afghanistan; and address the mental health concerns associated with such deployments.

According to the Department of Defense, as of March 2009, more than 123,843 Guardsmen and Reservists were deployed to Iraq and Afghanistan (Department of Defense, 2010b). In 2008 these troops comprised more than 35% of all U.S. forces in Iraq (National Veterans Foundation, 2008). This represents the largest deployment of citizen soldiers since World War II. Women currently comprise about 15% of the National Guard and 18% of reservists (Women in Military Service for America Memorial Foundation, 2009).

Upon demobilization, members of the National Guard and Reservists face unique challenges relative to health care not shared by active duty units. For example, active duty combat teams return to a base or fort as relatively intact units that have access to all of the bases mental health and other services while Guardsmen and Reservists are either reassigned to other units or are very quickly transitioned into the civilian environment which may or may not have the services that they need (Post Deployment Health Reassessment Program Task Force (PDHRA), 2007).

Also, because the onset of emotional or mental health disability symptoms is variable and unpredictable, symptoms may manifest themselves immediately or take years to appear. This is problematic for all combat veterans but particularly Guardsmen and Reservists who have between discharged and are no longer a member of a military organization. This issue is compounded because veteran enrollment in the VA system is not automatic and there seems to be insufficient command emphasis to ensure this action (e.g., completing and submitting VA Form 10-10EZ) takes place (PDHRA Task Force, 2007). Finally, sometimes Guardsmen and Reservists experience delays in receiving campaign awards, medals, and badges such as the Combat Action Badge (CAB) and the Combat Infantry Badge (CIB). This not only lowers their post-deployment morale but also can have a direct impact on whether they will receive significant federal VA benefits, entitlements and medical services since both the CAB and CIB verify a veteran's combat experience (PDHRA Task Force).

Counselor Interacting with Military Personnel

Civilian counselors are most likely to encounter younger veterans in career/ vocational counseling centers or settings. This will probably happen because many of the most recent veterans will seek to continue their education in college and will seek assistance in negotiating the college environment. Another reason is that talking with a career or vocational counselor will not have the same implications for the veteran that going to the counseling center of seeing a mental health counselor might have. Regardless of the veteran's motives, career and vocational counselors are most likely to be the first point of contact in civilian society for veterans.

Secondary Traumatization

Counselors cannot actually contract Post Traumatic Stress Disorder (PTSD) by working with veterans who have been diagnosed with PTSD though veterans themselves will sometimes joke about this. There are conditions, however, that are sometimes a consequence of prolonged trauma work. Counselors who work with either military or civilian trauma survivors commonly report experiencing a variety of posttraumatic sequelae similar to the experiences of their clients (Neuman &

Gamble, 1995). Somatic symptoms of headaches, nausea, and sleeplessness, intrusive images, having difficulty in trusting others, emotional numbing and sexual problems are common responses to trauma work (Neuman & Gamble). Some argue that these responses actually reflect the counselors' own pathology. However, the authors suggest that these symptoms represent a therapist's expected reaction to prolonged trauma work.

Several terms are associated with this phenomenon, such as, traumatic countertransference (Herman, 1992); secondary traumatization (Munroe et al., 1995); vicarious traumatization (Perlman & Saakvitne, 1995); or compassion fatigue (Figley, 1985). Figley defined this occurrence as a state of tension and preoccupation with the individual client or with the cumulative trauma of clients as manifested in a clinician in one or more of the following ways: (a) re-experiencing the traumatic events, (b) avoidance/numbing of reminders of the traumatic event and (c) persistent arousal. For the therapist, it involves the absorption and retention of the client's emotional suffering as it interacts with the therapist's own experiences, past and present and could lead to burn out. Neuman and Gamble (1995) add that it is a negative transformation in the therapist's inner experience that results from exposure to the client's traumatic material. This exposure can result in a disruption of the therapist's sense of identity, worldview, spirituality, ability to tolerate strong affect and his or her central cognitive schemas regarding safety, trust, control, and intimacy. If left unattended, the consequences to the therapist can be pervasive and can range from occasional non-empathic distancing from clients to victim blaming and progressive loss of energy and idealism.

Neuman and Gamble (1995) suggest that vicarious traumatization is related to countertransference and is often a precursor to burnout. Over time, vicarious traumatization produces emotional exhaustion, depersonalization, and reduced feelings of personal accomplishment, which coincide with the three (3) major components of burnout as conceptualized by Maslach and Jackson (1986). It is important to stress, however, that vicarious traumatization can be a normal response to the intensity of the trauma work and it is not an indication of incompetence on the part of the therapist. However, it does need to be addressed by the therapist through clinical supervision and/or consultation as well as through self care techniques.

McCann and Pearlman (1990) also suggest that vicarious traumatization is a more adequate concept than "burnout" or "countertransference" in describing what happens to therapists who begin to experience the internal lives of their traumatized clients. The therapist's cognitive schema about the self and the world are altered during the course of treating trauma survivors in such a manner as resulting in significant changes in the therapist's own thoughts, behaviors, feelings, and relationships. McCann and Perlman define schemas as the "cognitive manifestations of psychological needs" (p. 137). A therapist may experience either subtle or catastrophic disruptions in their schemas about self and world when working with trauma survivors depending on the degree of discrepancy between the client's traumatic memories and the therapist's existing schemas. Each individual's unique way of experiencing trauma depends upon which schemas are personally salient to him or her. As therapists learn more about their psychological needs, they will be able to process traumatic material more effectively and limit its impact upon their schemas (McCann & Perlman).

Friedman (2004) discusses three contexts relating to therapist vulnerability. First, there are those therapists who have never been traumatized themselves but become overwhelmed by what clients say during the course of treatment. They experience guilt, feelings of powerlessness, have rescue fantasies or exhibit numbing behaviors. The more symptomatic they become, the harder they work, and the less likely they are to seek assistance for their condition. Second there are those therapists who may experience countertransference reactions to client material and experience intrusive recollections of their own traumatic experiences. Finally there are those therapists who have been exposed to the same traumatic experiences as those they seek to assist. This last context is less likely to occur since very few civilian therapists have had combat experience. There may also be a combination of the above.

Neuman and Gamble (1995) report additional factors that may increase a counselor's susceptibility to being traumatized in their work with clients. These include: the level of professional status within the agency; the anxiety related to professional viability (as well as poor counselor self-efficacy); the lack of access to professional mentors or role models; and the therapist's own personal history of traumatization that has not been resolved or worked through by the therapist, where the therapist over identifies with his or her traumatized clients and struggles to maintain professional boundaries.

Professional Status and Therapist Self-Efficacy

Clinicians at the bottom of the organizational hierarchy (e.g., those newly hired or those with less experience) may also lack the collegial and technical support of their more seasoned colleges. This may be especially true for students and/ or interns. Status is also a mediating variable influencing the novice counselor's anxiety about his or her professional viability in the workplace. New professional counselors are particularly concerned about performance issues for both the sake of their clients' welfare and for their own economic security. These two status factors are also consistent with Cherniss' (1993) concept of professional self-efficacy which he defined as the professional's belief in his/her ability to effectively perform within three domains of professional work roles: Tasks, interpersonal relations, and organizational influence; where, tasks refer to the person's ability to perform the job duties; interpersonal relations refers to an individual's ability to work harmoniously with co-workers and clients; and organizational influence refers to the person's ability to influence the social and political environment in an organization.

Cherniss (1993) argued that those with high professional self-efficacy experience less job related stress than those with lower levels of professional self-efficacy. The individuals with higher self-efficacy are not only resistant to burnout but are also capable of changing work environments to promote less therapist burn out. Although Cherniss did not address vicarious traumatization per se, it seems reasonable to assume that finding ways to increase counselors' self-efficacy in working with the veteran population would also be worthy of exploration as a preventive strategy. In fact, Coll, Weiss and Draves (2010) have studied clinician perceptions of self-efficacy in working with veteran clients, and found that clinicians who were veterans themselves or spouses of veterans had higher levels of perceived self-efficacy than those clinicians who were not military related. The findings also indicated that those with experience in counseling military clients and having had continuing education in military related counseling courses also had higher perceived self-efficacy scores than those clinicians who had neither experience nor education.

Therapist Self-Care

Two common elements that therapists bring to assist in the treatment process are the need to help others and the need to demonstrate professional competence. An additional issue that may provoke feelings of inadequacy in the therapist is that the clients present with immense needs at multiple levels. In attempting to meet all of the client's needs, the therapist may over extend or become over involved with his or her client and this could contribute to therapist burn out. Professional counselors as a whole tend to derive meaning in their lives by helping others and trying to feel worthwhile [through] the client's appreciation and treatment gains. From a psychodynamic perspective, therapists often experience their client reactions as a mirror in which they (the therapist) can see themselves (Perlman, 1995). Ironically, the gifts and compliments that clients may bring to their therapist are also tokens of the client's need to be connected to the therapist and to avoid to the wrath of the therapist; the same wrath that has played a part in the client's significant relationships. Hence, when therapists see terror in their client's faces, they come to believe and feel that they must be doing something wrong or are in some way hurting the client. This in turn evokes shame and guilt in the therapist. It is then that the therapist's own counter transference may cause him or her to actually respond in anger protesting (and possibly rejecting) the perception of the client rather than exploring these issues more deeply. The combination of the therapist's need for emotional fulfillment and the client's need for interpersonal attachment can become most confounded and can also contribute to sexual feelings and/or behaviors in the therapeutic relationship (Perlman). Thus the author suggests that therapist's ability to oscillate between emotional connection and intellectual analysis will enable them to use both empathic immersion and intellectual perspective in guiding their behavior with clients (Perlman, 1995). Thus the essential task of the therapist is to engage the client at his or her deepest level of despair without becoming self absorbed to the point of denying the clients reality or failing to hear the client's voice because his or her words have become too threatening for the therapist.

Specifically when working with veteran clients counselors need to be aware not only of their own trauma experiences and their psychological reactions to their clients but they also need to examine their attitudes and biases about working with the military population (Coll, Weiss & Draves, 2010). This is not only an aspect of culturally competent services (viewing the military as a subculture), but also perhaps as another component to prevent burn out (which could be further studied). For additional information see Coll, Weiss and Draves' (2010) study that examined the impact of civilian counselor war attitudes (OIF & OEF) and their perceived self-efficacy in working with veterans.

Self-Care Tips

(Adapted from Pearlman and Saakvitne, 1995, p. 150; Yassen, 1995, p. 205)

- Identify disrupted schemas (in the areas of personal safety, trust, esteem, intimacy, & control)

- Maintain a personal life (maintain a balance between work and life)

- Use personal psychotherapy for support

- Identify healing activities (relaxation, exercise, creative expression, meditation, humor, sleep, nutrition)

- Tend to your spiritual needs

- Obtain supervision/consultation/mentor

- Seek peer support

- Set boundaries/limit setting

- Set up a coping plan and evaluate it (weekly and monthly goals)

- Educate self/develop skills

- Engage in social action

Issues That Bring Military Personnel to Counseling

Psychological Trauma

There are several questions or rather clusters of questions that you might consider related to trauma. We could begin with, what do we mean by "trauma"? What makes an event traumatic and what does it mean to say someone has been traumatized? The word trauma is borrowed from medicine and refers to a sudden and dramatic tissue loss and a violent disruption of normal functioning in one or more organ systems. Psychological traumas also involve sudden negative changes in an individual's normal level of functioning. For our purposes, we will define a trauma as a severe disruption and/ or failure of an individual's ability to tolerate, assimilate, or accommodate an event or the report of an event into an individual's cognitive schema.

Trauma, itself, is highly subjective for at least two reasons. First it is not possible to determine who will experience a trauma and second, it is not possible to know the specific characteristics of an event that will result in psychological or emotional trauma for a given individual. The Diagnostic and Statistical Manual of Mental Disorders, 4th Edition, Text Revision (American Psychiatric Association, 2000) has attempted to define a traumatic event in terms that capture the essential elements of all traumatic events. Criterion A for posttraumatic stress disorder (PTSD) defines a traumatic event as one that involves actual or threatened death or serious injury or a threat to the physical integrity of self or others and results in a response of intense fear, helplessness, or horror (American Psychiatric Association, 2000).

Although this is a very good definition, it still does not solve the problem of the subjective experience of the individual. Events that are inherently dangerous and could result in great bodily harm (e.g., being chased by several bulls through the streets of a small city in Spain) might cause intense fear in some individuals but result in excitement for others. The definition also does not explain why individuals would be fearful of the threat of injury or death to another person (Carlson, 1997) nor does it explain why some individuals feel no anxiety or fear while watching injury occur to others or death and sometimes even enjoy the experience. Hence the question still remains regarding what causes an individual's response of intense fear, helplessness, and horror.

Carlson (1997) has attempted to address this question by describing three defining elements that will elicit the responses described in the second half of the DSM-IV definition of traumatic events. These elements are (a) "the perception of the event as having a highly negative valence", (b) "the suddenness of the experience", and (c)" the individuals inability to control events and the subsequent threat to the individuals physical safety and psychic integrity" (Carlson, 1997, p. 28).

Perception of the Event as Negative

The first of the three critical elements that cause an experience to be traumatic seems to be very clear. An event that is physically painful or injurious, or that is emotionally painful, or that is perceived as likely to cause physical pain or injury, emotional pain or death would logically be perceived as negative. Carlson (1997) points out that the likelihood of physical or psychological pain, injury or death may be traumatizing even if the events do not actually occur. Carlson also notes that the perception of the event is more important than the actual danger associated with the event, and negative valence is an important causal factor in producing a traumatic response. However, the factors that cause the negative valence of an event to surpass the threshold and cause trauma are not clearly understood (Carlson). It therefore remains difficult to predict with any degree of certainly which events will be perceived to be traumatic for a given individual.

Suddenness

Events that pose an immediate threat are more likely to precipitate overwhelming fear than those that occur gradually (Carlson, 1997). The critical factor is the amount of time between the individual's awareness of danger and the occurrence of the danger itself because that is precisely the amount of time that the individual has to either act or to cognitively integrate the event (Carlson, 1997). The amount of time needed to process an event differs from individual to individual but it would seem that the likelihood of avoiding a traumatic response to an event increases if one has weeks, months, or years to adjust to a negative event (Carlson).

Lack of Controllability

Lack of controllability is the third critical defining feature of traumatic events. Protection from physical harm is a fundamental aspect of human survival (Carlson, 1997). Hence, individuals seek to control their immediate environments to the extent that they perceive possible painful experiences (physical or psychological) in that environment. Controllability and predictability are also related because predictable events are more likely to be controlled than unpredictable events. Thus, whether an event is predictable or not, "it will be traumatizing if it is experienced as uncontrollable and sufficiently negative" (Carlson, 1997, p.33). As in negative valence, uncontrollability must also reach a certain threshold in order to cause traumatization (Carlson).

These characteristics are all mediated through perception and therefore require a certain threshold to be surpassed before an event will be experienced as traumatic. Carlson also notes, however, that even if an experience is sufficiently negative, sudden, and uncontrollable and perceived to be potentially traumatizing, a posttraumatic response may not occur if the effects of the event are modulated by "favorable" individual and situational factors. These factors include, an individual's psychological and physical resilience, an individual's cognitive and emotional developmental level at the time of the trauma, the severity of the trauma, the social context for the individual both before and after the trauma, and the life events that occur prior to and subsequent to the trauma.

The military response to war zone induced psychological trauma

The psychological consequences of the war zone experience may be immediate, acute, or chronic (Litz & Orsillo, 2003). Immediate consequences refer to the psychological sequelae and impairments in functioning that occur during battle or during exposure to other war zone stressors (Litz & Orsillo). The symptoms of an acute war zone stress reaction include restlessness, psychomotor deficiencies, stuttering, confusion, nausea, vomiting, withdrawal, and extreme suspiciousness and distrust in others (Litz & Orsillo).

The military response to psychological consequences of the war zone experience follows a continuum that begins with prevention. Currently, military officers are taught to utilize post battle debriefing to allow troops to vent their feelings and emotional reactions as a way of preventing internalized stress reactions and enhancing morale and unit cohesion (Litz & Orsillo, 2003). Debriefing is not counseling and officers are not expected to engage in counseling. A second level of intervention might involve a recommendation for a soldier to participate in pastoral counseling.

Subsequently, if a commander determines that a soldier ceases to function militarily as a combatant, and acts in a manner that endangers himself or his or her fellow soldiers, the soldier will be relieved of duty and evacuated from the battle area to receive rest and critical incident stress debriefing or in some cases formal psychiatric care (Litz & Orsillo, 2003).

The principle that underscores the military's response to treating the psychological consequences of war zone experiences is known by the acronym, "PIES," which stands for: Proximity, Immediacy, Expectancy, and Simplicity (Litz & Orsillo, 2003). This principle was utilized with soldiers both during World War I and II (Sheppard, 2000). The principle suggests that early intervention be provided as close to the soldier's unit as possible with soldiers being assured that their reactions are normal and are expected to return to their units shortly. They also receive food and rest to help counteract the effects of physical exhaustion. Although few U.S. service members actually become psychiatric casualties of war, a few soldiers do return to the U.S. with serious war-zone induced psychotic disorders (Litz & Orsillo)

Posttraumatic Stress Disorder (PTSD)

The DSM-IV-TR groups the symptoms of PTSD under three headings: B (intrusion) the event is persistently re-experienced in one or more of five possible ways; C (avoidance) stimuli associated with the traumatic event are avoided and accompanied by numbing of general responsiveness; and D (disordered arousal) persistent symptoms of increased arousal as indicated by at two of five possible ways (American Psychiatric Association, 2000). However, even if a person has all the symptoms of PTSD he or she cannot be diagnosed with PTSD unless he or she meets Criterion A (i.e., exposure). As previously stated, PTSD is defined as an individual having been exposed to an event that involved the actual or threatened death or serious injury, or the threat to the physical integrity of self or others AND the person's response involved intense fear, helplessness, or horror (American Psychiatric Association, 2000). If criteria A through D have been fulfilled and have persisted for more than one month, a diagnosis of PTSD is made. If the symptoms have persisted for less than one month the diagnosis of Acute Stress Disorder (ASD) should be considered instead (American Psychiatric Association, 2000).

The National Center for PTSD notes that posttraumatic stress disorder has been diagnosed in 31% of men and 27% of women Vietnam veterans (Price, 2007). There have been a multitude of studies conducted on prevalence rates of PTSD among those veterans who have served in Iraq and Afghanistan, with most results ranging from 5%-20%. Those deployed to Iraq have are more likely to report PTSD symptoms than those deployed to Afghanistan, likely due to more frequent combat exposures (Ramchand, et al., 2010). A study conducted by the RAND Corporation found that nearly 20% of Iraq and Afghanistan veterans report symptoms of Post Traumatic Stress Disorder or major depression. Of these service members, slightly more than half actually seek care for their symptoms (Ramchand, Karney, Osilla, Burns, & Caldarone, 2008).

Most veterans will not develop PTSD yet a considerable amount will at some point in their lifetime experience PTSD symptoms. Causes of PTSD reactions occurring to some people in traumatic situations and not everyone cannot be explained however, it is important for the client to understand that if he or she develops PTSD they are not weaker than others in their situation (Department of

Veterans Affairs & National Center for PTSD, 2002). Clients with PTSD seem to be frozen in time and are continually re-exposed to the traumatic event through daytime recollections that persistently interrupt ongoing thoughts actions or feelings (Friedman, 2004). He or she may have reoccurring nightmares about events witnessed, actual combat situations, and reliving an actual combat situation (Hyer, McCranie, & Peralme, 1993). Such intrusive recollections can persist over 50 years and may get worse rather than better over time (Friedman). On occasions the clients take on too much responsibility in trying to make sense of situations that occurred during combat and subsequently experiencing emotions such as survivor guilt and self blame. Developing avoidant/numbing symptoms towards the intolerable emotions and memories stirred up these intrusive recollections.

Clients with PTSD also suffer from autonomic hyperarousal. They are always on guard, dedicated to avoiding re-exposure to terrifying circumstances that changed their lives. They also isolate themselves as they are "on guard" and find it difficult to trust others or the environment. Their need for safety and protection outweighs all other considerations including intimacy, socialization, and other pleasurable pursuits. Often a veteran's sleeping patterns may be disrupted and getting a full night's rest becomes difficult and stressful. Concentration and staying on task in regular activities may also be affected when the client is dealing with Acute Stress Disorder or PTSD. In addition, clients are affected with post-combat adjustments within the family structure. He or she should not feel obligated or expected to discuss their combat experience with family members or others (National Center for PTSD, 2005). They need to relearn the feeling of safety, comfort, and trust towards loved ones before re-engaging.

Clients' anger and irritability may be stimulated easily since he or she is physically tense and feeling as if they have no control of their lives. Anger is a natural emotion that can be expressed in either healthy or unhealthy ways (National Center for PTSD, 2005). Aggressive behavior can cause relationship problems in areas such as marriage, interpersonal relations, and employment tribulations. Byrne and Riggs (1996) found that combat exposure was related to veterans' use of aggression against their partners. Veterans with higher levels of PTSD symptoms experience more frequent and severe relationship problems (Byrne & Riggs). Engaging in hazardous and disruptive behavior are frequent symptoms that cause service members impacted by TBI and/or PTSD to incur criminal and legal problems (Burke, Degeneffe, & Olney, 2009). Veterans Affairs estimates that veterans account for 10% of people who have criminal records (Leinwand, 2009). It is important to remind clients that he or she has a support network to help them cope with their PTSD symptoms.

Treatment essentially involves asking the client to give up the protective barriers and psychological strategies that they have used to stabilize themselves. Since treatment is actually potentially destabilizing, clients may get worse before they get better. Because of the high rates of co-morbidity between PTSD and other mental disorders, the trauma history is the major vehicle through with PTSD can be distinguished from other major mental disorders (Friedman, 2003, p. 3).

There are several assessment devices for PTSD. Included here is the Primary Care PTSD (PC-PTSD), a quick screen is typically used by physicians to detect PTSD.

PC-PTSD

In your life, have you had any experiences that were so frightening, horrible, or upsetting that in the past month, you...

1. Have had nightmares about it or thought about it when you did not want to?

2. Tried hard not to think about it or went out of your way to avoid situa tions that reminded you of it?

3. Were constantly on guard, watchful, or easily startled?

4. Felt numb or detached from others, activities, or your surroundings?

Answering in the affirmative to any three of these items is considered "positive" for PTSD and indicates the need for further assessment (Prins et al., 1999). See Appendix A for other assessment devices

Military Sexual Trauma (MST)

Many counselors might assume that PTSD symptoms will be the main reason a veteran becomes motivated to seek counseling. However, PTSD is only one of the many different ways a veteran may manifest readjustment difficulties. Veterans are at risk for depression, substance abuse, aggressive behavioral problems and other mental illnesses induced by the war zone experience (Litz & Orsillo, 2003). Another major issue for returning veterans may be military sexual trauma (MST). Military sexual trauma refers to both sexual harassment and sexual assault that occurs in a military setting (Street & Stafford, 2003).

Both men and women may be victims of MST and the perpetrator can be of the same or opposite sex and/or a fellow comrade. In the 2009 fiscal year there were a total of 3,230 reports of sexual assault involving military service members as either victims or subjects; this was an increase of 11% from 2008. Eighty-nine percent of sexual assault victims who filed unrestricted reports that led to completed investigations were female, while eleven percent were male. For those victims that filed restricted reports of sexual assault, 87% were female and 11% were male (Department of Defense Sexual Assault Prevention and Response Office, 2010). Filing a restricted report allows the victim on a confidential basis to disclose details of the assault only to specified individuals. In these cases, law enforcement is not informed, nor does the command structure become involved, thus eliminating the possibility for disciplinary or protective action (U.S. Army, 2005). If the victim chooses to file an unrestricted report they receive medical treatment including a forensic examination, counseling, and they can inform the appropriate legal and/or command authority; the advantage of unrestricted reporting is that the notification of law enforcement and the command structure allows actions can be taken to protect the victim (U.S. Army, 2005).

Sexual assault of male soldiers also takes place but the reported incidence is very low (Coxell & King, 2002). Coxell and King suggest four myths about sexual assaults among men that may account for this. These are that:

1. Men cannot be forced to have sex

2. Men who sexually assault other men must be gay.

3. Erection and/or ejaculation imply that the man was in some way complicit.

4. A man who is sexually assaulted by another man must himself be gay or must have been behaving in a "gay" manner. (pp. 52-54).

Even though most men probably believe they would exhibit strong physical resistance to a sexual assault, Coxell and King report that "freezing"—or passive submission-- is actually the most common victim response.

Hodge and Canter (1998) also state that sexual assault of men by strangers is significantly more likely to be perpetrated by heterosexual men. Coxell and King (2002) further state that an erection and/or ejaculation does not mean the victim of the assault enjoyed the experience. Erection and ejaculation can be involuntary, but since the majority of male victims of sexual assault do not know this, they are further distressed by the belief that they actually could be gay. Health professionals, friends, and family members may also share one or all of these beliefs (Coxell & King). Since survivors of sexual assault may not always volunteer their status, it is important to include a sexual history as part of the counseling process for all combat veterans.

Sexual trauma that is associated with military service may occur during basic training, during stateside active duty, or during war zone deployment. It is most likely to occur in settings where the victim lives and works and in most cases the victim continues to live and work with her or his perpetrator (Street & Stafford).

Many victims are reluctant to report sexual victimization for several reasons. First, perpetrators are frequently peers or supervisors responsible for making decisions about work related evaluations and promotions. Thus the victim is placed in the position of choosing between their careers and their safety. Second, many victims believe there is no safe way to report sexual victimization. Many believe their reports would either be ignored or be told to keep quiet and even be accused of fabricating a report (Street & Stafford, 2003). Finally, because unit cohesion is so highly valued in the military, victims are often unwilling to make negative reports regarding other service members (Street & Stafford).

Screening and Assessment

In 2004, the Department of Defense established the Sexual Assault Prevention and Response (SAPR) Office to develop a comprehensive policy. The recommendations of the SAPR Office have resulted in drastic changes in DoD policy to include services such as restricted reporting options for victims. Since 2005, the Department has developed prevention strategies, increased reporting, improved care and response to victims, implemented program oversight, and expanded knowledge of the Sexual Assault Prevention and Response program among service members (Department of Defense Sexual Assault Prevention and Response Office, 2010).

It is important to screen all veterans for a history of sexual harassment and sexual assault. Male and female veterans are frequently reluctant t0 volunteer any information regarding whether or not he or she has encountered harassment and assault. A sensitive, compassionate screening should be carried out for a veteran who may have experienced sexual trauma (Street & Stafford, 2003), as stigma is often attached to this association, especially in male victims.

Street and Stafford (2003) mention that disclosure upon the topic of sexual harassment and assault depends on the feeling of shame and self-blame a veteran is experiencing. It is noteworthy to avoid terms like "rape" and "sexual harassment" during the screening because this assumes the person knows how these terms are defined (Street & Stafford, 2003).

Street and Stafford (2003) suggest two general questions that could serve as a brief assessment:

1. While you were in the military, did you ever experience any unwanted sexual attention such as verbal remarks, touching, or pressure for sexual favors?

2. Did anyone ever use force or the threat of force to have sex with you against your will?

Although Street and Safford (2003) do not use this question, one additional question might be added to the brief assessment:

3. Did anyone every give you alcohol or any other type of drug that caused you to be incapable of resisting someone having sex with you?

The last question may help to gain responses from male victims of sexual assault who would other wise not respond because they were not "forced."

Treatment

Counseling for sexual trauma involves addressing immediate health and safety concerns, normalizing post-trauma reactions, providing the victim with validation, and facilitating the development of new coping skills (Street & Stafford, 2003).

Treatment may also include cognitive restructuring and exposure therapy to deal with the fear, self-blame, shame, anger and disillusionment that accompany victimization. In general, it is important to remember that the emotional responses of combat veterans are complex and may seem somewhat paradoxical. Most notably, the range of emotions accessible to traumatized veterans is often limited (Smith, 1985). Hence, one of their major tasks in counseling will be to identify their feelings and to learn to express a range of emotions (Smith). T he second phase of counseling combat veterans involves helping veterans to learn to tolerate the conflicting emotions they experience, and ultimately to understand the emotional responses of their family members and other members of civilian society. The final phase of counseling involves helping veterans develop a civilian as well as military identity. Furthermore, treatment should involve addressing immediate health and safety concerns (Street & Stafford, 2003).

Traumatic Brain Injury

Soldiers serving in Afghanistan and Iraq are surviving injuries that probably would have been fatal in earlier wars for two basic reasons. First, they are better protected by Kelvar helmets and ceramic body armor and second, they are receiving improved emergency medical treatment in the field as well as much better rapid evacuation services to hospitals (Miller, 2007). Although body armor prevents many fatal penetrating wounds to the chest, abdomen, and back and sides of the head, it, unfortunately, does not protect arms, legs, necks and faces as well. These parts of the body remain vulnerable, and blasts and explosions from artillery, bombs, grenades, and roadside bombs have wounded more U.S. soldiers than any other hostile action during the war in Iraq (Miller, 2007).

According to the Department of Defense, as of early December 2006, more than half of the U.S. soldiers killed in action during the war in Iraq died as a result of an explosion. Preliminary research by the Department of Defense and by the U.S. Department of Veterans Affairs' Brain Injury Center indicates that about 10% of all troops in Iraq and up to 20% of infantry troops suffer from concussions as a result of IEDs and other explosives (National Veterans Foundation, 2008).

Explosions are particularly harmful to the brain and may damage it in several ways. First, soldiers may crash their heads against buildings or the ground after been thrown into the air by the force of an explosion. Second, the blast may hurl metal fragments or other objects against or into the service member's skull causing penetrating wounds requiring surgery to remove these projectiles and to control infections. Finally, service members standing close to the source of the blast will experience a sudden wave of high pressure that can fracture the skull and bruise the brain sufficiently to cause it to swell and bleed (Miller, 2007a). This is particularly serious since swelling of the brain may result in a coma: a condition in which the higher brain functions stop leaving only the basic functions of the brain stem operating.

Although a service member exposed to an explosion or to a series of explosions may experience only a momentary loss of consciousness and may show no obvious head trauma such as changes in thinking, he or she may still have sustained a serious closed-head injury. In fact, the impact of the injury may not be recognized at all while the service member is in the war zone. Accordingly, many service members may first experience the symptoms of traumatic brain injury (TBI) such as frequent headaches, short-term memory loss, sleep disturbance, confusion, irritability, repeated nausea or vomiting, shortened attention span, slower-thinking, and depression only upon redeployment. Ironically, since many of these symptoms are also consistent with those of Post-Traumatic Stress Disorder (PTSD), the presence of TBI (which may be a co-occurring condition) may be overlooked.

Research on the prevalence of TBI among retuning troops is sparse, possibly because of methodological restraints. Although identifying penetrating brain injuries is straightforward, estimating the prevalence of closed-head injuries and primary blast injuries is difficult. Symptoms of mild TBI also overlap with those of other conditions such as PTSD (Ramchand, Karney, Osilla, Burns, & Caldarone, 2008). The Armed Forces Surveillance Center reported 178,876 total service members with Traumatic Brain Injury since 2000 (Defense and Veterans Brain Injury Center, 2010).

Suicide

Unfortunately, many veterans due to their acute stress and depression attempt suicide and often are successful. Suicide is currently the 11th leading cause of death in the United States and substantially outnumbers homicides, with 1 suicide occurring every 16 seconds.

The Military Mental Health Advisory Team III found that the suicide rate for military personnel serving in Iraq and Kuwait in 2005 was 19.9 per 100,000 members compared to the 18.8 rate in 2003 and the 13.0 rate in 2004 (Harben, 2006). The greatest suicide risk factors included problems with fellow military members, military job performance, issues with legal actions, and personal relationship difficulties. The Military Mental Health Advisory Team found that the suicide rate for military personnel servicing in Iraq and Kuwait in 2005 was 19.9 per 100,000 members (Harben, 2006). Comparatively, non-veterans in 2005 killed themselves at a rate of 8.9 per 100,000 (Burke, Degeneffe, & Olney, 2009). In the fiscal year 2009, 160 Army soldiers took their own lives, making suicide the third leading cause of death among the Army population. There were also 1,713 suicide attempts (Army, 2010). From the years 2001 through 2009, the number of suicides within the Army, Marine Corps, and Navy all increased significantly. In 2009, within the Marine Corps the rate reached nearly 25% (Army, 2010). When the circumstances behind these deaths were investigated, a direct link was found between increased life stressors and increased risk behavior. For some service members life stressors included the rigors of service, repeated deployments, injuries, separations from family (resulting in a sense of isolation, hopelessness, and life fatigue), and a permissive unit environment (Army, 2010).

Veterans are two times at greater risk than civilians and account for 1 in 4 suicides within the US. In 2007 the associated press and the US Army reported the highest rate of suicides among soldiers in 26 years with a quarter of the suicides occurring while serving in Iraq and Afghanistan.

It is critical that counselors become aware of who is at risk for suicide, which is everyone and we should never assume. However, highest risk factors are those who have:

1. Reported suicidal ideations

2. Reported suicidal intentions

3. Reported a suicidal plan

Specific warning signs to be aware of are:

1. Hopelessness

2. Rage, anger, seeking revenge

3. Reckless or impulsive behaviors

4. Isolation

5. Increasing alcohol and drug use

6. Anxiety, agitation, insomnia

7. Dramatic changes in mood

8. Feeling trapped

9. No reason for living

When working with Veterans who have suicidal ideations it is important to provide them with the National Suicide Hotline Number 1-800-273 TALK (8225). They should be instructed to prompt #1 for veterans or family of veterans, which will connect them with a 24 hour VA mental health staff.

Substance Abuse

Substance use is a large concern among the military. Aggregated data from the Substance Abuse and Mental Health Services Administration's annual household survey reveal that from 2004-2007, 7.1% of veterans met criteria for a past-year substance use disorder (National Institute of Drug Abuse, 2009). Problems with alcohol and nicotine abuse are the most prevalent and pose a significant risk to the health of veterans. Those at greatest risk are deployed personnel with combat exposures as they are more apt to engage in new-onset heavy weekly drinking, binge drinking, and to suffer from alcohol-related problems. Reserve and National Guard personnel, in addition to younger service members are particularly vulnerable to subsequent drinking problems (National Institute of Drug Abuse, 2009).

Past research has suggested that veterans report higher rates of alcohol abuse than non-veterans and are more likely to meet the criteria for alcohol abuse and dependence than non-veterans (Disabled American Veterans, 2008). In 2000, more than 55,000 veterans, the majority of whom were male, were admitted to substance abuse treatment (Substance Abuse and Mental Health Services Administration, 2001).

According to an Army Post-Deployment Reassessment Study completed in 2005, alcohol abuse among soldiers rose from 13% among all soldiers to 21% (after one year) among those soldiers who were returning from Afghanistan and Iraq (National Veterans Foundation, 2008). Also, approximately 20% of the veterans of the wars in Iraq and Afghanistan who received care from the VA between 2001 and 2005 were diagnosed with a substance abuse disorder (National Survey on Drug Use and Health, 2008).

A 2007 Army study found that alcohol misuse was a problem that service members were willing to report and that alcohol overuse was a potential problem for many veterans after returning from combat. This study also suggested that opportunities exist for early intervention to prevent alcohol problems (U.S. Army, 2008). Accordingly, substance abuse is likely to be either a presenting problem or a co-occurring disorder among many veterans returning from deployment in Afghanistan and Iraq.

Intimate Partner Abuse and Child Abuse

Family violence may be more common in the military population compared to the civilian population because of higher overall stress levels associated with the military lifestyle such as frequent separations, long work hours, and a dangerous work environment (Rentz et al., 2006). In a literature review conducted on abuse in military and civilian populations, it was concluded that spouse abuse is more prevalent and more severe in military families compared to civilian families (Rentz et al., 2006). Estimates of Intimate partner violence (IPV) committed by Veterans and active duty servicemen range between 13.5% and 58%, which is up to three times higher than those rates for civilians (National Center for PTSD, 2010). The National Center for PTSD reported that women veterans and active duty military personnel are more likely than non-veterans to have experienced IPV. Thirty-nine percent of women veterans were found to have experienced IPV at some point in their lives. For active duty women, 30-44% reported having experienced IPV during their lifetimes (2010). Research suggests that IPV rates are higher among veterans with PTSD than among veterans without PTSD or than individuals in the general population (Scioli, Otis, & Keane, 2010).

In first year post-deployment OIF/OEF war veterans' trauma symptoms significantly predicted lower marital satisfaction in the veteran and partner within the first year post-deployment (Sadler, 2009). It was also found that recently returned military veterans with depression and/or PTSD are five times more likely to have problems with family adjustment than veterans without these diagnoses (Sayers, Farrow, Ross, & Oslin, 2009).

Polytrauma

Polytrauma originally referred to the combination of traumatic brain and other system injuries that resulted from exposure to a single blast. It has been revised to include any combination of multiple bodily systems that can be injured in a single event, not necessarily including brain injury (Uomoto & Williams, 2009). Advances in field medicine and protective equipment for vital organ systems have resulted in a high percentage of soldiers surviving physical injuries that would have been fatal in past conflicts which results in high percentages of soldiers returning home with polytrauma (Scioli et al., 2010). War-injured service members with polytrauma and pain often suffer from extensive, multisite tissue wounds complicated by significant TBIs, frequent surgical revisions or extensions, lengthy tissue healing periods, altered physical appearance, sensory loss, limb amputation, emotional trauma, and the activation of multiple pain systems (Uomoto & Williams, 2009).

Themes in Therapy

Smith (1985) suggests there are four major themes that characterize therapy with combat veterans who suffer from PTSD: control, integrity, ambiguity, and personal accountability. All may not be represented in every case, and some may emerge at different times during the course of therapy. Although these themes were first identified in Smith's work with Vietnam –era veterans, they remain relevant for working with combat veterans of other wars.

Control

Fear of losing control of their feelings and behavior often prompts veterans to seek counseling (Novaco, 1996; Shay, 1995; Smith, 1985). Veterans may report unpredictable mood swings, or rage and homicidal ideation during seemingly minor incidents. Smith states that a veteran's fear of "going off" should always be taken seriously. It is especially important to ask if the veteran is concerned about the use of a weapon during an incident of "going off." Smith suggests that fear of losing control and reverting to some kind of brutal nature is often related to some past action that the veteran views as an atrocity or as a major violation of his or her moral code. Essentially, the veteran is concerned, consciously or unconsciously, about repeating this act. In order to avoid losing control, veterans will often isolate themselves from others and consciously avoid social situations. Although veterans typically view this behavior as a necessary means of preventing their loved ones from experiencing their outbursts, their friends and family members typically interpret the veterans' behavior as a form of rejection.

Counseling strategies related to helping veterans maintain their sense of control should be directed toward the presented situation rather than the underlying cause. The core components of treatment consist of cognitive restructuring, arousal reduction procedures, and behavioral rehearsals with the therapist (Novaco, 1996). Gerlock (1996) states that the guiding principles of successful anger management interventions for veterans are acceptance of responsibility and accountability. The primary tasks for the therapist include helping veterans gain a sense of control over events through discussing the event, helping them identify the points at which their anger begins to escalate, and helping them develop alternative modes of action (Novaco, 1996; Smith, 1985).

Integrity

This theme seems to focus on conflicts related to justice, fairness and morality and usually arises as criticism or blame directed toward the government, an institution, a group of individuals, or a particular individual (Smith, 1985). Examples include attacks on the federal or state government regarding their lack of concern regarding veterans' affairs or attacks on civilians for not understanding the meaning of Memorial Day or Veterans Day, or attacks on the Veterans Administration for poor health care services. Smith interprets these conflicts as a veteran's means of coping with some perceived failure to act decisively or appropriately or to some act of cowardice or self-preservation that resulted in the death or injury of someone else. Thus, the anger and blame projected onto others masks the shame or guilt the veteran may feel for his or her own actions. An alternative way to think about this theme is that the veteran is struggling with conflicts he or she has experienced between the ideals that attracted him or her to military life and the actual experience of military life. This happens because the military exists to protect an ideal and largely romanticized version of American life, and service members enlist not to protect the America that actually exists, but to protect the America that is supposed to exist (Wertsch, 1991). The conflict between what veterans thought they were going to do and feel versus what they actually did and felt is very often a source of extreme disillusionment for them.

Ambiguity

The theme of ambiguity means veterans consistently expressing contradictory or seemingly incompatible attitudes towards the war zone experience (Smith, 1985). Examples include statements about hating the enemy on the one hand and statements about the beauty of the land and the people on the other or statements about being used as a pawn of the government versus feelings of patriotism and duty. One of the most important goals of counseling is for veterans to come to recognize and integrate their feelings of honor and futility as well as their feelings of joy and sorrow (Smith). Ideally, during the course of therapy, veterans will be able to develop the cognitive schemas that will allow them to process and integrate the entire war zone experience and not just selected parts of it.

Personal Accountability

Personality accountability is, perhaps, the most powerful and overarching theme expressed in the war zone narratives of combat veterans. Smith (1985) states that personal accountability is by far the most critical issue in significant cases of PTSD, and at the core of most cases of combat –induced PTSD is a veteran's belief that she or he acted incorrectly and caused a tragic or deadly outcome. This subjectively perceived responsibility for what did or did not happen is the source of intense shame, guilt and pain for many combat veterans, and it is one of the most difficult cognitive distortions to reframe. The difficulty rests in the fact that the veteran views the incident in the present with the full knowledge of what happened in the past but from only one perspective (his or her own) while rejecting the fact that he or she could have not known the future at the time of the incident.

The basic themes of control, integrity, ambiguity and personal accountability seem to permeate the war zone narratives of many combat veterans and also suggest some of the underlying feelings and thoughts that motivate veterans' behavior. Recognizing these and other themes as well as the cognitive distortions that accompany them, will assist counselors and other mental health professionals s as they work with veterans to construct effective treatment goals and strategies.

Assessment of a Clinical Case Involving Sexual Trauma and Initial Treatment By Carmen T. Stein-McCormick, Ph.D., LMHC Department of Psychological and Social Foundations, University of South Florida

Susan is a 40-year-old female professional. She denies any known family history of mental problems or substance abuse. Susan was in the military for 6 years and is currently married to her third husband. She is high achieving and has always set very high goals for herself, which she has always achieved. Susan has very good coping skills, but is somewhat rigid in her expectations of herself.

Susan presented with complains of feeling "unsatisfied," irritable and devoid of sexual desire for her husband of whom she admits loving very much. She also stated she has tension headaches that often turn into migraines as well as periods of sadness which usually pass quickly (30 minutes or less). Susan stated that she often feels like a failure because of her three marriages, even though she has been very successful at everything else. When asked about her military experiences, she was quick to offer examples of her "sexual trauma" during her military years and shared that she was constantly "harassed and sexually taken advantage of by the males in the military." She attributed her sexual abuse by men to her "ignorance and immaturity" as well as to her early childhood sexual abuse. However, Susan does not ruminate over her childhood sexual abuse, but harbors extensive anger towards the men in the military who had abused her.

Susan stated that she joined the Army when she was 19. She reported coming from a very protective Mid-western family. When she joined the Army, she was assigned jobs in which there were few other women. This was typical of the 1970s. Within the first month of arriving at her work station, she was approached by the Battalion Executive Officer (XO) who was very nurturing and "made her life very easy". This friendship very quickly changed into a sexual relationship that was mutually agreed upon by both parties. However, Susan was a 19 year old Private First Class female, and the XO was a 35 year old male Major. The rank and age difference plus Susan's past history of sexual abuse placed her in an extremely vulnerable position; one of not knowing how to say "no". This relationship continued for about 6 months until the XO was transferred to another unit because of his outstanding performance during his current assignment. Within 3 months, Susan was approached by her orthodontist who was taking care of her teeth. They began a sexual relationship that continued for about 1 year. During both these sexual relations Susan reported experiencing depression as well as memories of her childhood sexual abuse.

Susan attempted to get an appointment with the mental health clinic on base to discuss her depression. However, these appointments were very difficult to get because she would have to report to "sick call" first between 6:00-6:45 am and then have to go through the Battalion headquarters (where the Major had worked) and state why she needed to go to sick call. Since she was not willing to do this, she knew "this was not going to work".

Soon after the second affair ended, Susan became pregnant with her first child by her first husband who was also in the Army. The pregnancy ended in a miscarriage, and Susan said she used the miscarriage to finally speak with a Mental Health professional.

She was given an appointment to speak with the psychiatrist who very quickly told Susan that she was having a "neurotic reaction" to her miscarriage. He then showed her how to do relaxation exercises in his office. Susan recalled that she had been very aware of the time she went into the psychiatrist's office. She stated that she left about 1 hour later, but she had the feeling there was time for which she could not account. Susan told me that she is convinced that the psychiatrist "put [her] under hypnosis" and did something to her because when she woke up from her "relaxation exercise" she had an overwhelming feelings of disgust and shame. The psychiatrist terminated the session by telling Susan "everything will work itself out".

(Continued)

Susan went on to have numerous affairs during her Army career but none that she instigated. All her affairs were one-sided, with the males being the aggressor. Susan said she would then have to find ways to avoid these men, just as she had to do as a child. Susan stated, "how do you turn in your boss for being a pervert? I didn't know I could refuse him." Four years into her career Susan's first husband divorced her because she had lost interested in sex with him.

The Army never followed-up on Susan's adult sexual trauma, and Susan believed the VA viewed her sexual trauma as being treated best by "leaving it in the past" since she was separated from the service. Susan suffered from intermittent depression with anxiety symptoms, and she attempted to get help for this from the VA but to no avail. Susan reported going once a year to the VA and each year being told to "make an appointment with the social worker who will evaluate [your] 'present needs' ".

Susan filled out the Beck Depression Inventory (BDI) for me and scored 15, which is indicative of mild depression. Her preliminary DSM-IV diagnosis was Depressive Disorder Not Otherwise Specified (311.00), given that her episodes were recurrent but brief lasting from 2 days up to 2 weeks and occurring at least once a month but not related to her menstrual cycle. Susan also had some symptoms of anxiety that we discussed and eventually attributed to depression.

Due to Susan's high level of cognitive functioning as well as her high motivation to overcome her past trauma, I chose to approach her diagnosis through Cognitive-Behavioral Therapy (CBT). Susan seemed to be an excellent candidate for CBT, which could help her to improve her affect as well as some of her maladaptive thinking. Before we began treatment, Susan and I agreed that if her symptoms became worse, we would consider a psychiatric evaluation for antidepressant therapy. I chose to apply CBT from a Feminist Framework given that Susan was a very high functioning female with somewhat assertive tendencies. I believe the therapeutic alliance was established so quickly in this case because of Susan's motivation and because I was a woman who also had prior military experience.

Susan felt very comfortable and opened up immediately in the next session sharing all of her "secrets" and was able to release some of her anger as well as remove the emotionality from her early childhood sexual trauma. Susan terminated therapy after six sessions indicting reduced symptoms as well as increased interest in sexual relations with her husband. She came back three years later for what she called a "tune up" for another three sessions. During these sessions I concentrated on having her recognize how safe her present husband was for her and also recognize that she needed to learn to trust herself as well as her husband.

(Continued)

Some of her last comments to me were that this "new sexual relation" she had with her husband was something she had always wanted but was ashamed to pursue. Susan shared that even though she and her husband had been married almost 15 years, "this new sexuality" she was now experiencing was "for the first time without fear and or guilt".

Susan was an excellent client. She was very bright and very willing to explore her trauma. Her husband did attend two of her sessions during which she shared with him the childhood sexual trauma as well as her military sexual trauma. She now sends me many military referrals including males who had been sexually traumatized.

Case 2

The setting is a community mental health center in a large metropolitan area in the Midwest. The client is Melvin Johnson, an African American male combat veteran from the Vietnam Era. The intake sheet gave his age as 59 though he appeared to be in his late 40s. Only his grey hair suggested that he might be older. He is over six feet tall, weighing approximately 200 pounds and was appropriately dressed for an autumn day. His trousers were sharply creased and his shoes were highly polished. He was a self-referral and a walk-in. He knew about the mental health services that the Veterans Affairs (VA) Hospitals provided, but he said, "All they want to do is give you either a test or some pills." He stated his presenting problem as "just needing to talk to someone." He was assigned to an African American male counselor who was also in his 50s but a little younger than Mr. Johnson.

Csl-1:   How do you do Mr. Johnson. I'm Harold Evans and I'll be working with you (They shake hands and the counselor points in the direction of his office). We will be meeting back there. Would you like some coffee?

Melvin: No thank you.

(The counselor walks into his office and Melvin follows)

Cal-2:   Please sit in this chair next to the door if that is alright with you.

Melvin: Do you know anything about working with veterans?

Csl-3:   I have worked with veterans before but I'm not a veteran myself. I'm a civilian. I haven't had any military service. By the time my number came up, Nixon had ended the draft. I don't work for the VA and I'm not in the chain of command.

(Continued)

Melvin: I wish I had stayed in school. I had a football scholarship. I don't know what got into me but I had to join Army. Well, that's not really true. The first time I saw an Army Ranger with that black barret and those split shinned combat boots, I knew I had to be one of those guys. That's really why I joined up.

Csl-4:   So you were a Ranger?

Melvin: Yea. They dropped us off back in the boonies to train those ARVN who were never worth a damn.

Csl-5:   How long where you in?

Melvin: I did two tours but I was in the service for 20 years. I worked at the post office for the next 10 years, then I had to quit because of the pain in my left arm, my back and my left leg. One of those ARVN hit a trip wire and blew up half the platoon. It caught me all along my left side. It I had not been standing next to a tree I would have been gone too. There is still shrapnel in my back. The doctors said it was too close to my spine to try to remove. The good part was that I got shipped back state side and I finished out my 20 as an instructor.

Csl-6:   I'm glad you made it back, too. I a lot of the fellas I knew never made it back. So when you left the post office did you go on disability?

Melvin: Yea. They gave me 80% for my arm leg and back and 50% for PTSD.

Csl-7:   So you're 100% total and permanent?

Melvin: That's right. Total and permanent.

Csl-8:   And how is your PTSD?

Melvin: The medicine takes care of everything. I don't have nightmares anymore, and I have an easier time dealing with civilians. I couldn't even have come in here after I left the Army. Just couldn't deal with civilians. I knew something was wrong but I couldn't pub my finger on it. But I'm going to get off these drugs. They're just a crutch, and I don't think they're doing me that much good anymore.

Cal-9:   I could see how you might feel that way. It's hard to tell if the drug is working if you feel fine.

Melvin: That's what I mean. I don't think that it makes sense to have to take drugs for your whole life. At the VA they told me that PTSD is a permanent condition and that you can never get well. I don't believe that. Do you believe that's true?

(Continued)

Csl-10: I believe that people get better over time. Some more than others. I know that some people have fewer and less severe symptoms than others, but I don't know of a case where there was a combat veteran that had been diagnosed with PTSD and all of this symptoms suddenly disappeared. I'm not saying it couldn't happen. I just saying I've never seen it happen. I'm also saying that if you decide to stop taking your meds, you should let your doctor at the VA know that right away. Sudden withdrawal could have some serious side effects for you.

Melvin: I'm still thinking about doing it.

Csl-11: I understand but please keep you physician informed. Well, Mr. Johnson, I guessing that you did not come here to talk with me about your meds. How can I help you today?

Melvin: The problem I'm having is with my wife.

Csl-12: Alright.

Melvin: She keeps telling everyone that I'm crazy and that she waiting for me to die.

Cl-13: How long has she been doing this?

Melvin: Ever since she retired from the school system.

Cls-14: And how long has that been?

Melvin: For the last five years.

Csl-15: Can you give me an example of how this would come up in a conversation?

Melvin: Well, yea. Say if she's talking to our son on the phone, she'll start talking about, "You know how your daddy is," and "You know he's got that PTSD and you don't know what he'll do next."

Csl-16: And how does your son respond to that?

Melvin: He just ignores it because he knows it not true. I'm not saying there was never a time when I wasn't like that but that was 10 years ago. But I'm tired of her calling everybody she can think of and telling them I'm crazy.

Csl-17: So if I understand this, you're telling me that for no reason—at least that you can think of –your wife calls your friends and relatives to tell them that you are crazy and unpredictable?

(Continued)

Melvin   That is exactly what I mean.

Csl-18:   I suppose you have confronted her about this.

Melvin: I told her if she ever did it again, that I would divorce her. I told her that three weeks ago.

Csl-19:   and what happened?

Melvin: She stopped for two weeks but then my son called me yesterday and told me she had started again. He told me he didn't know why I put up with her and that she needed help.

Csl-20:   Well, then, what do you want to happen?

Melvin: I want her to go somewhere and get some help or I'm going to see my lawyer.

Discussion

Older African Americans also have counseling needs. Couples are not always happy married for a variety of reasons. Many times they were never happily married, but married out of convenience or necessity. Other times they may have not been happily married at one time but currently. Yet they may have chose to remain together, to at least occupy the same house, " for the sake of the children" or to avoid the stigma that was once associated with divorce. This stigma is not so present in contemporary African American communities.

There two aspects of this case that make it noteworthy. The first is that the actual presenting problem was not revealed until fairly late in the session. There were many opportunities for the counselor to rush to foreclosure and to assume the client's issue had to do with PTSD just because the client was a Vietnam Era combat veteran. The other issue is that the counselor had to demonstrate trustworthiness and cultural sensitivity in a domain other than race or gender. The salient variables in this case were race, age, and military experience.

It is important to remember that the training, socialization, and indoctrination military service members experience along with the lifestyle that they have are different enough from civilian life to warrant the term military culture. It is also important to remember that there are a fairly large number of veterans in the U.S. Thus, the likelihood of civilian counselors having veteran clients will continue to increase.

According to the 2000 U.S. census there were 26.4 million veterans in the U.S. This means that veterans accounted for 12.7% of the adult population. Vietnam Era veterans, 8.4 million, accounted for the largest populations of veterans in 2000, and nearly 33% of all living veterans are from that Vietnam -Era. World War II veterans make up the next largest group with approximately 5.7 million members or 21.7% of all veterans (U.S. Census Bureau, 2003).

Although the number of male veterans has declined, the number of women veterans has continued to increase. Approximately 10% of veterans who served from May 1975 to August 1980 were women, and approximately 13% of those who served from September 1980 to July 1990 were women (U.S. Census Bureau, 2003). From August 1990, approximately 15% of veterans have been women.

The counselor in this case was familiar with these facts and also familiar enough with military culture to give an answer (Csl-3) that would be acceptable to Melvin. I t was important for the counselor to say that he did not have connections with the VA because many veterans are not happy with the services they received from the VA. It was also important for him to mention "chain of command" because it lets Melvin know that the counselor has some knowledge about the military and it also lets Melvin know that whatever he might say to the counselor will be held in confidence.

The next set of counselor questions (Csl-4—Csl-7) were designed to get a quick assessment of Melvin's military experience in preparation for the question (Csl-8) that directly address the issue of Posttraumatic Stress Disorder. Since Melvin was not only a deployed veteran but also a member of an elite combat group, it was very appropriate to ask about PTSD. Melvin's question about PTSD was not a test question. He was genuinely interested in getting a second opinion regarding the course of PTSD. The counselor's answer (Csl-10) addressed several issues that may not be immediately apparent.

First it addressed the issue of being disabled. Being disabled is difficult for many African Americans to accept. Whatever the disability may be older African Americans in particular believe that they should be able to overcome it either alone or through God's help. Physical disabilities are more readily accepted than mental disabilities because they are visible. They can be seen by other members of the community and validated as an unfortunate event. Mental disabilities, however, are still sources of shame, and the stigma associated with them is to the affected individual's family as well as to the affected individual. Melvin has the additional pressure of being not only a member of the military but also a member of an elite military unit. The notion of a mental disorder for him is very likely perceived as a sign of mental weakness and unmasculine behavior; neither of which are acceptable.

Second it addresses Melvin's ambivalence about having a disability status classified as "total and permanent." On the one hand, he receives enough income to be able to retire from the post office, but on the other being totally and permanently disabled his not how he actually feels each day. He feels that the 80% disability rating he received for his physical wounds is honorable, but he does not feel as honorable about the 50% rating for PTSD (disability ratings may total more than 100% but they are only compensated up to 100%). Finally, the counselor seeks to give Melvin some encouragement for his recovery but at the same time reminds him that he should not make medical decisions without consulting his physician.

The next set of counselor statements (Csl-11—Csl-19) focus on defining the problem, and the last question (Csl-20) begins the discussion of how Melvin would like the problem to be resolved. The counselor would continue the interview in this manner until he had clarified Melvin's goals and he and Melvin would have developed several culturally acceptable strategies for helping Melvin.

Treatments

Treatment modalities for working with veterans

Returning veterans may present with a number of different issues, some may stem from acute stress reactions to the war zone experience. A second set of issues may be related to the process of veterans readjusting to the civilian world including managing their relationships with friends, family, school or the workplace. Regardless of which set of issues veterans present with, counselors can provide education, coping skills training grief support and family counseling as necessary. Specifically for the treatment of post traumatic stress disorder and associated problems or co-occuring disorders (i.e., depression or substance abuse) counselors should be aware of several evidence based interventions, such as, Cognitive Processing Therapy (CPT); Prolonged Exposure Therapy (PE); and Eye Movement Desensitization Reprocessing (EMDR). Pharmacological treatment through appropriate physician referral may also be indicated.

Treatment essentially involves asking the client to give up the protective barriers and psychological strategies that they have used to stabilize themselves. Since treatment is actually potentially destabilizing, clients may get worse before they get better. Because of the high rates of co-morbidity between PTSD and other mental disorders, the trauma history is the major vehicle through with PTSD can be distinguished from other major mental disorders (Friedman, 2004, p. 3).

Education

The educational aspect of care should focus on helping veterans recognize and understand their symptoms as well as reduce fear and shame relative to their symptoms by normalizing their reactions to severe stress. Education should also explain the recovery process to veterans so that they will feel less out of control regarding their symptoms. Education should focus not only on explaining PTSD but also on the homecoming process and the various adjustments that the veteran might expect to experience.

Coping Skills Training

Coping skills training is designed to help veterans regain a sense of personal control over their emotions. Coping skills training may focus on anger management, anxiety and stress management, interpersonal communication and /or emotional grounding. The counselor should help the veteran decide which areas to focus on for skill development based on the issues that the veteran is facing. In general, coping skills training should focus on helping veterans learn how to do the things that will support their recovery (Ruzek et al., 2003). Effective coping skills training is based on a cycle of instruction that includes education, demonstration, role-played rehearsal with feedback and coaching, and between-session real world practice with self-monitoring notes.

Grief Support

Pavlicin (2007) states that "grief is a way a person responds to and works toward acceptance of a loss" (p.112). The author adds that it is natural for service members to form attachments to their comrades in their units and/or to others who have participated in their missions and many veterans have experienced the loss of fellow soldiers. Counselors can aid veterans with their bereavement by educating them on stages of grief denial, bargaining, anger, depression, and acceptance (Kubler-Ross, 1969). Counselors can assist the veteran client to reconstruct or re-create meaning out of death experience by re-authoring the narrative associated with the loss (Neimeyer, 2000; White & Epston, 1990); reduce feelings of guilt in the veteran which often appears in the form of survivor guilt by replacing faulty cognitions ("If only I would have done something differently, my comrade would not have died") through techniques such as cognitive-behavioral interventions (Beck, 1976) or through Acceptance and Commitment Therapy (Hayes & Smith, 2005), the acceptance of human suffering and the use of mindfulness and values based living.

Family Counseling

Family counseling recognizes that veterans are part of a larger unit than themselves and that readjustment issues distress both the veteran and his or her family. Veterans' successful recovery and reintegration often hinges on consistent long-term family support. It is very important that all family members have an understanding of what is happening, why it is happening and what it will take for things to get better. Family counseling may include family education, couples counseling, family therapy, parenting workshops, and/or conflict resolution skills training. Support for the veteran and the family can increase the potential for the veteran's eventual reintegration into family life and reduce the likelihood of future problems (Ruzek, et al, 2003). The next chapter will further explore military family issues and working with veterans and their families.

Cognitive Processing

Cognitive Processing Therapy (CPT) (Monson, Schnurr, Resick, Friedman, Young-Xu & Stevens, 2006; Foa, Keane & Friedman, 2000) is designed to help clients challenge negative and self-defeating thoughts and is one of the best-validated treatments for PTSD. It is a specific form of cognitive-behavioral therapy based on a manualized 12-session treatment protocol (and can be delivered in a group format). This approach helps veterans learn about the relationship between thoughts, events and emotions and the negative beliefs held by veterans regarding their war zone experiences. The most useful aspect is that it helps veterans develop alternative interpretations about their thoughts which then influence their feelings.

Dialectical Behavior Therapy

Dialectical Behavior Therapy (DBT) focuses on helping patients modify their ways of thinking and behavior (Mason & Kreger, 2008) by teaching clients to focus on the present and use effective, healthy means of coping with distress (Linehan & Heard, 1992). Fundamental concepts of DBT include: clients are doing the best that they can, clients are motivated and willing to change, radical acceptance is essential to recovery, and mindfulness is key to managing emotions (Mason & Kreger, 2008). When working with veterans and/or active duty military, DBT can be used to teach alternative coping methods to decrease the frequency of painful and provocative events prompted by affective distress. By providing veteran clients with a variety of alternative approaches, a mental health counselor could stem further increases in acquired capability and thus diminish the likelihood of a client engaging in unhealthy behavior (Anestis, Bryan, Cornette, & Joiner, 2009).

Motivational Interviewing

Motivational Interviewing (MI) is an evidence-based, client-centered method that facilitates exploring and resolving the ambivalence that keeps many people from making desired changes in their lives. In MI, responsibility for change is left with the client and a great respect is given for the individual's autonomy. Four broad guiding principles underlie motivational interviewing: express empathy, develop discrepancy, roll with resistance, and support self-efficacy (Miller & Rollnick, 2002). MI can be used to treat combat-related PTSD symptoms in veterans (Murphy, 2008), as a framework for the treatment of depression, for those reluctant to seek treatment, and during treatment for those with whom problems in motivation arise (Arkowitz & Westra, 2009).

Exposure Therapy

Prolonged Exposure therapy (PE) (Foa, Hembree & Rothbaum, 2007) is designed to help veterans confront their trauma- related emotions and memories. It involves having veterans repeatedly verbalize the incidents that trouble them until their fear responses are consistently diminished (through habituation and extinction). Exposure therapy may also be conducted in vivo by having veterans visit areas or attend situations that symbolize the traumatic experience. Virtual Reality (VR) exposure therapy is another variation in the utilization of this model which is based on a human-computer interaction within a virtual environment in a three-dimensional world (such as Iraq and Afghanistan) giving a sense of being immersed in the virtual environment (Rothbaum, Difede, & Rizzo, 2008). All forms of exposure therapy are usually conducted in conjunction with education, coping skills training, and cognitive processing.

EMDR

Eye Movement Desensitization and Reprocessing (EMDR) originated by psychologist, Francine Shapiro, Ph.D, has been extensively researched and recommended as a prime intervention for trauma (Shapiro, 2001). This method of treatment has been endorsed by the American Psychiatric Association (2004) and by the Department of Defense and Veterans Affairs (2007). It is an integrative psychotherapy approach that utilizes the brain's Adaptive Information Processing (AIP) system with bilateral stimulation (or dual attention stimulation through eye movements, taps or tones) along with a strong cognitive-behavioral component to modify the negative emotions associated with the trauma into more positive ones. For more detailed explanation of the model as well as research on outcome data please refer to the aforementioned author and organizations.

Pharmacological Treatment

This form of treatment is typically provided by physicians or other mental health professions that prescribe psychotropic drugs. Combined treatment, coordinated between psychiatrists and therapists, however, is probably most effective in managing the systems associated with PTSD, and promoting the readjustment of the veteran. For at least this reason, it is important that counselors and other mental health professional to be familiar with medications (along with their actions and side effects) that are typically prescribed for war zone induced psychological disorders. The following section will review this topic in more detail.

In general, pharmacological treatment for acute stress reactions (within one month of the trauma) is reserved for soldiers who remain symptomatic after having received brief crisis-oriented psychotherapy (Ruzek, et al, 2003). The U.S. military is currently attempting to avoid unnecessary use of medications for stress-related symptoms. Once a decision has been made to use medications for acute stress reactions, a brief (four days or less) course of treatment with benzodiazepines is typically recommended. (Ruzek, et al, 2003). Benzodiazepines are also prescribed to veterans for co-morbid anxiety symptoms and for sleep initiation (Raskind, 2009).

A different course of pharmacological treatment, however, is recommended for chronic PTSD clients. Several classes of medications are used to aid in the treatment of combat veterans. These include: (a) serotonin reuptake inhibitors (SSRIs), (b) beta-blockers, (c) low-dose anti-psychotics, and (d) mood stabilizers.

Prazosin is an effective and well-tolerated treatment for trauma nightmares, sleep disturbance, and global clinical status in veterans with chronic PTSD. Prazosin has been used safely for many years in general medicine to treat hypertension and urinary outflow obstruction caused by benign prostatic hypertrophy (Raskind et al., 2007). It has been theorized that patients with recent trauma may respond to a lower dosage than those with a more distant trauma (Miller, 2008).

Serotonin Specific Reuptake Inhibitors (SSRIs)

The mechanism of action of the SSRIs is thought to be the inhibition of the absorption of serotonin, the neurotransmitter most associated with enhancing mood (Faiver, Eisngart, & Colonna, 2000). The SSRIs that are typically prescribed for veterans include: Fluoxetine (Prozac), Sertraline (Zoloft) and Paroxetine (Paxil) (Davidson et al., 2005).

Some studies suggest that SSRIs benefit for the majority of PTSD symptoms but they demonstrate little or no benefit for trauma-related nightmares and sleep disturbances. Common side effects with SSRIs include nausea, loose stools, headache, insomnia, and agitation with initial treatment, and weight gain and sexual dysfunction over the long term (Davidson et al., 2005). As of 2004, SSRIs were prescribed to 85% of veterans with a PTSD diagnosis given any psychotropic drug by the VA. It has been proposed by Raskind (2009) that such widespread use in the VA despite negative studies and guideline recommendations suggests that VA clinicians detect symptomatic benefit from SSRIs in their chronic PTSD patients. The symptoms that appear most likely to benefit from SSRIs are co-morbid depression and anxiety and PTSD "irritability/low anger threshold."

Main effects

One main effect of Prozac on combat veterans diagnosed with PTSD is that it helps in anger management, and self-mastery of anger leads to an increase in self-respect for most veterans (Shay, 1995). It allows them more time to think before they act, and it does this without sedation or otherwise altering the veteran's consciousness (Shay). The duration of aroused anger is also much shorter. Most veterans feel humiliated if the explode in angry rather than handling situations another way. Fear of these outbursts or "going off" is also one of the reasons veterans avoid social situations and isolate themselves. Hence, the greater sense of self-control Prozac affords provides relief from this humiliation and increases the likelihood of increased withdrawal and social isolation.

In addition, Prozac seems to have a direct anti-depressant effect for combat veterans (Shay, 1995). The paradox with all antidepressants is that they have been known to give chronic depressed patients the energy to kill themselves (Shay). Hence, veterans who try to rebuild their lives without the support of family, other veterans, and therapy might try to kill him or herself during the periods of despair that accompany readjustment. This, however, is a risk for anyone who recovers from a severe depression (Shay).

Side effects

Prozac and the rest of the SSRIs do have side effects, and these drugs do not work well for everyone. Common side effects include anxiety, dizziness, insomnia, and sexual dysfunction. A less common side effect (but particularly relevant to veterans) is unusual or vivid dreams (Faiver, Eisengart, & Colonna, 2000). Although lithium is perhaps most well know for its role as a mood stabilizer in managing bipolar disorder, low doses, e.g., 600mg/day, are effective in helping some veterans maintain their self control when angry and this may be an alternative for veterans who cannot tolerate Prozac (Shay, 1995).

Beta Blockers

Beta-blockers were originally developed to treat hypertension and cardiac arrhythmias, but are now also prescribed for anxiety (Faiver, Eisengart, & Colonna, 2000). The beta-blocker that is most typically prescribed to combat veterans is propanolol (Inderal) (Evers, 2007).

Main effects

Beta-blockers assist in anger management by lowering blood pressure and slowing the heart to block the physical effects of adrenalin on the body (Shay, 1995). They interrupt the mind-body-mind cycle in rage reactions. An example of how this cycle operates is the following example.

A veteran hears a statement or observes an action that he or she perceives to be offensive. First, the veteran's cognitions are filled with rage nearly instantly. Second, the veteran's body responds with adrenalin that make the heart pound, the muscles tense and the stomach burn. Third, these bodily sensations in turn restrict the veteran's perceptual field and reasoning ability and signals to the veteran that combat is imminent. Shay states that the "roar of the adrenalin" drowns out all thought about other options.

Many combat veterans, however, do not like losing the "roar". Some say that these medications weaken them because they associate being pumped up with adrenalin with their personal strength (Shay, 1995). They do not like the feeling of "losing their 'edge'"; loosing the feeling of being a warrior. It is true that if a veteran is over-medicated with one of these drugs, she or he will actually feel weaker because of unstable blood pressure, but this feeling does not persist with the correct dosage (Shay).

Side effects

Beta-blockers also have side effects. Common side effects include depression, fatigue, sedation, and sexual dysfunction (Faiver, Eisengart & Colonna, 2000). Perhaps the most salient side-effect is that massive overdoes can be fatal by slowing the heart so much and subsequently dropping blood pressure so low that the brain does not get enough blood flow (Shay, 1995). Accordingly, beta-blockers should never be taken with alcohol.

Low-Dose Neuroleptics (Anti-psychotics)

Neuroleptics or anti-psychotics are typically used to treat psychosis. Symptoms of psychosis may include delusions, hallucinations, aggression, agitation, and impaired reality testing. Atypical anti-psychotics have recently begun to be used to treat PTSD; PTSD trials suggest potential benefits of this drug class for PTSD sleep difficulty, irritability/anger outburst, intense flashbacks, and comorbid psychotic symptoms in veterans. Drugs in this category include: Risperidone, Olanzapine, and Quetiapine (Raskind, 2009).

Main effects

Raskind (2009) cautions that when using atypical anti-psychotics there is an increased risk for the metabolic syndrome which must be taken into account when deciding if and when they are appropriate for the long-term treatment that is often necessary for chronic PTSD. Drugs in this category are essentially sedatives (Shay, 1995).

Side effects

Common side effects are substantial weight gain, dyslipidemia, elevated blood glucose, and the metabolic syndrome (Raskind, 2009).

Mood Stabilizers

Mood stabilizers are designed to alleviate the symptoms of mania and hypomania and to stabilize the mood fluctuations of bipolar disorder. They are also used to treat aggression, impaired thinking, impulsivity, and panic attacks (Faiver, Eisengaart & Colonna, 2000). Drugs in this category include Lithium (Eskalith), Valporic Acid (Depakote), Carbamazepine(Tegretol), and Clonazepam (Klonopin).

Main effects

Mood stabilizers stabilize the mood fluctuations, impulsivity and impaired thinking associated with mania, hypomania, bipolar disorder, and panic attacks. They are also used to treat aggression.

Side effects

Mood stabilizers are associated with a set of serious side effects so clients taking these medications must be monitored closely (Faiver, Eisengart & Colonna, 2000). Common side effects for this category include dizziness, dry mouth, blurred or double vision, and drowsiness (Faiver, Eisengart & Colonna). More severe side effects include liver failure with use of Depakote and death by lithium overdose.

Other Drugs

Trazodone (Desyrel) and Nefazodone are anti-depressants but are prescribed to some veterans to help them sleep without experiencing horrible nightmares (Raskind, 2009). Trazadone has also been prescribed to offset SSRI-induced insomnia (Ruzek. Curran, Friedman, Gusman, et al, 2003). Mirtazapine, another anti-depressant has shown some benefit for treating PTSD symptoms but can produce daytime sedation and weight gain (Davidson et al., 2003). Quinine usually associated with managing malaria is also sometimes prescribed to help veterans sleep without thrashing about wildly during the night. It helps to control "sleep jerks" (nocturnal myoclonus).

Drugs veterans should avoid

There are several drugs that may have adverse side effects for veterans. Shay (1995) suggests the following should be avoided:

1. Benzodiazepines. This class of drugs has less of a risk for overdone and fewer side effects than the barbiturates so they are often prescribed for anxiety (Faiver, Esingart & Colonna, 2004). This category includes drugs such as diazepam (Valium), alprazolam (Xanax) and lorazepam (Ativan). As noted previously, these drugs are often administered to veterans displaying symptoms of acute stress reactions because they are effective in reducing extreme arousal and anxiety and help to improve sleep (Raskind, 2009). Shay (1995), however, does not recommend these drugs for veterans because of their side effects.

First, they produce a rebound effect: a temporary worsening of the symptoms of the disorder. Second, benzodiazepines have been associated with short-term memory loss (Faiver, Eisengart,& Colonna, 2000; Shay, 1995). Third, this class of drugs can cause excessive sedation with an accompanying risk of falls and other accidents (Faiver, Eisengart & Colonna, 2000). Fourth, drugs in this class have the potential for creating dependency and addiction (Faiver, Eisengart,& Colonna, 2000; Shay, 1995). Finally, as Ruzek, et al, (2003) note prolonged use (two or more weeks) of benzodiazepines may contribute to acquiring PTSD symptoms. In general, benzodiazepines should not be recommended for veterans with PTSD (Ruzek, et al, 2003; Shay, 1995).

2. Caffeine. The positive effects of caffeine are well known. Feeling more alert, energetic, and optimistic are all positive effects of caffeine. Less well known, however, is that caffeine may also cause anxiety and depression (Shay, 1995).

The reason this can occur is because caffeine is actually more than one drug, and an individual may not react to all three drugs in the same way.

The caffeine that enters the body through coffee or a soft drink for example is converted into theobromin, which is subsequently converted into theophyllin (Shay, 1995). The peak effects for these drugs are approximately two hours for caffeine, four hours for theobromin and six hours for theophyllin. The issue is that thousands of people may have good reactions to caffeine but adverse reactions to theobromin or theophyllin. This means that the initial burst of energy and optimism that follow a cup of coffee could be replaced by anxiety and depression four to six hours later. Since either caffeine or one of its metabolites may contribute to anxiety and depression, as well as poor sleep, Shay suggests that it be avoided.

3. Yohimbine. Yohimbine is an herbal product available at most health food stores and vitamin shops that is used in the treatment of male impotence. The reason that it is contraindicated for veterans with combat induced PTSD is that it induces flashbacks and panic attacks (Davis, Barad, Otto, & Southwick, 2006; Shay, 1995).

The advent of Viagra and other related drugs has lessened the likelihood that a veteran experiencing erectile difficulty might use Yohimbine, but clients should be warned of the potentially dangerous side effects of using this herbal remedy.

4. All Other Illegal Drugs. The most obvious reason to avoid these drugs is that they are illegal and running the risk of being incarcerated does not help veterans reintegrate into civilian society. Use of illegal drugs may expose veterans to dangerous people and situations that could trigger PTSD symptoms. Also the pharmacological properties of illegal drugs may not be known and a veteran could have a serious adverse reaction to the drugs.

5. Alcohol. Although Shay (1995) does not list alcohol as a drug to be avoided, drinking alcohol is not advisable for veterans diagnosed with PTSD for several reasons. First, the likelihood of an adverse reaction with some other medication is extremely high. Second, alcohol increases disinhibition and increases the probability that the veteran will engage in impulsive behavior. Third, excessive use of alcohol could lead to alcohol dependence, and finally alcohol interferes with the veteran's ability to access his or her repressed feelings and thoughts.

A Treatment Process

Friedman (2004) suggests that therapy can be divided into three phases:

1. Establishing trust and safety

2. Exploring traumatic material in depth

3. Disconnecting the client form the trauma and reconnecting him or her with the family, friends and society.

In each phase it is important to find and emphasize each veteran's strengths in meeting the challenges of readjustment to civilian life. Marmar, et al (1995) have suggested that there are five identifiable post-traumatic syndromes each requiring a different treatment. These are:

1. Normal stress response

2. Acute catastrophic stress reaction

3. Uncomplicated PTSD

4. PTSD co-morbid with other disorders

5. Post traumatic personality (Complex PTSD).

The normal stress responses occur in individuals in response to a discrete traumatic incident. Such individuals usually achieve complete recovery following individual or group debriefing through some method such as critical incident stress debriefing (CISD). Debriefing involves (a) and exploration of the survivors emotional responses to the event (b) and open discussion of the symptoms that have been precipitated by the event (c) presentation of information designed to normalize the responses of the survivors and (d) the identification of adaptive coping strategies (Friedman, 2004).

The acute catastrophic stress reaction is characterized by panic reactions, cognitive disorganization, disorientation, dissociation, insomnia, paranoid reactions and incapacity for fundamental self-care (Friedman, 2004). Treatment involves immediate support and in the case of soldiers, removal from the scene of the trauma, the use of anxiolytic medications for immediate relief of anxiety and insomnia and brief supportive psychotherapy (Friedman, 2003).

Uncomplicated PTSD involves the classic DSM symptoms that define PTSD. The symptoms are treated with a variety of approaches but primarily a combination of cognitive behavioral methods (exposure therapy and cognitive restructuring) plus psychopharmacological treatment. Group psychotherapy and psycho-educational groups are effective treatment approaches. In many ways the peer group setting provides an almost ideal therapeutic milieu for trauma survivors (Friedman, 2004).

PTSD Co-morbid with other DSM Axis I disorders is actually much more common than uncomplicated PTSD (Friedman, 2004, p. 6). Posttraumatic Stress Disorder is usually associated with at least one other major mental disorder such as depression, substance abuse or panic disorder. In fact, the other disorder is sometimes the presenting problem of the veteran. In general, the best results are obtained when both the PTSD and the other disorders(s) are treated concurrently. Friedman (2004) notes this is especially true for PTSD and substance abuse. The treatment approaches outlined for uncomplicated PTSD are also appropriate for these clients (Friedman).

Complex PTSD is found among individuals who have been exposed to prolonged traumatic experiences such as torture survivors, prisoners of war, or survivors of childhood sexual abuse. Individuals in this category often display behaviors that meet the criteria for a DSM Axis II disorder; impulsivity, aggression, sexual acting out, self-destructive behaviors, depression, fragmented thoughts, and dissociation characterize this group of clients (Friedman, 2004). Treatment generally focuses on behavioral and affect management, social skills training, alcohol and or drug rehabilitation, and family integration (Friedman, 2004). Trauma work should only begin after substantial   preparation and inpatient treatment may be needed to insure adequate safety for the client.

In summary, most soldiers do not become psychological casualties in the war zone although acute stress reactions are very common after exposure to severe trauma in combat (Litz & Orsillo, 2003). Most of these soldiers adapt and recover their normal functioning. Nonetheless, they are at risk for "chronic mental health problems implicated by experiences during battle" Litz & Orsillo, p.3). Some veterans may return to civilian life with an acute stress reaction that meets the criteria for Acute Stress Disorder (ASD) and are therefore at risk for the development of PTSD. The majority of veterans do not suffer from the symptoms of PTSD, but a significant percentage of combat veterans do have PTSD. The National Vietnam veterans Readjustment Study (1990) suggested that 15% of male veterans and 8.5% of female veterans had PTSD. Rates were higher among African American (27.9%) and Latino (20.6%) than among white (13.7%) veterans. Rates for veterans of the First Gulf War have been reported as 9.4% in men and 19.8% in women (Friedman, Schnurr, & MacDonagh-Clyde, 1994). Among service members currently deployed to Iraq and Afghanistan PTSD prevalence rates range from 5%-15% (Ramchand, Karney, Osilla, Burns, & Caldarone, 2008).

Interacting with Families

Preparing for the return of loved ones who have been deployed

What Families Should Know

Career military families will already know much of what we are about to say because they have experienced it. Other military families, for example those of Reservists or National Guardsmen, have their own unique experiences. Hence, one of the most important things that counselors and other mental health professionals can do is to educate family members about what to expect from their returning veterans. The following is an example of the type of information that could be discussed during a workshop or distributed as a flyer or pamphlet.

-----Title-----

Members of the armed forces that are deployed in a war zone frequently have serious reactions to what they have seen and experienced. Sometimes these reactions continue after the service member returns home from the war zone. Some of these reactions may include:

Nightmares or difficultly sleeping

Unwanted distressing memories or thoughts

Anxiety and panic

Irritability and anger

Feeling numb or detached

Using alcohol or other drugs to cope with stress

(Continued)

- A returning war veteran may feel irritable and have difficulty with communication, making him or her hard to get along with.

- A returning veteran may lose interest in sex and feel distant from his or her spouse or partner.

- A returning veteran may experience a loss of interest in family and social activities

- Veterans often feel that something terrible may happen (for no apparent reason) and can become preoccupied with trying to keep themselves and family members safe.

- The returning veteran may have lost his or her ability to be emotionally close and as a result family members may feel rejected.

These are all typical symptoms of traumatic stress reactions. If your loved one seems to be experiencing any of these symptoms, please have him or her contact your local Vet Center, VA, military medical facility, or family physician.

If you would like more information about traumatic stress reactions please feel free to contact me. ----Your name---- and ---phone number, or ----e-mail address---------

What Counselors Should Know

Returning home after deployment can be a wonderful and joyous event, but homecoming is much more complex than merely returning to the U.S. from abroad. The manner in which veterans experience homecoming can be vastly different depending on whether they return in groups or alone, or whether their military operation was public or covert, and especially whether their operation enjoyed favorable support from the civilian public. Veterans' status as career military, Reservists, or National Guardsman as well as their physical health and mental health will also influence how they will experience reunification. In addition to the issues related to how individual veterans experience redeployment, there are also the issue related to how military families experience redeployment and homecoming.

Deployment and redeployment are common events in military families and one of the characteristics of military families that distinguishes them from most civilian families. The cycle of separation and reunion that characterizes military culture and the impact that it has on military families is important for counselors and other mental health professionals to understand when we consider the meaning of homecoming. For this reason we will discuss the stages of this cycle that precede homecoming first and then return the topic of preparing for homecoming at the end of the discussion.

The Cycle of Separation and Reunion

Depending on the branch of the armed forces involved, there are from four to six stages that cover the processes of separation and reunion among service members and their families. These stages include pre-deployment, deployment, sustainment, re-deployment, and post-deployment (Kennedy, 2004). Each one of these stages has its own set of stressors and each possess different challenges to the service member and his or her family. The pre-deployment stage begins once the service member receives order to deploy. The time of deployment may be as little as a few days for active duty service members and possibly a few months for members of the reserves. In either case preparation for mobilization disrupts family routines, increases fear and anxiety within the household, and sometimes precipitates social withdrawal between the service member and other family members (Kennedy, 2004).

Deployment involves the actual separation of the service member from the family. One aspect of deployment involves the service member's process of adjusting to the war zone environment. The other aspect involves the family's adjustment to the service member's absence. Older children may act out and challenge boundaries as they try to cope with the separation of the service member (Kennedy, 2004). The younger children may regress and lose skills they had previously mastered. Any old family problems or issues may again resurface due to increased emotional tension within the family. The major challenges for the non-deployed parent are to establish a new family routine, management of family resources, and provide additional emotional support to the children all under conditions of uncertainty.

Kennedy (2004) states that the next stage, sustainment, lasts from the end of the first month of deployment until the month prior to service member's return. Sustainment is the period during which the service member and the service member's family accept their new roles (with varying degrees of success) and establish their new and independent daily routines. This is also the period during which the stressors of the war zone take their greatest toll on the service member and when the service member and the family are most separated physically and emotionally. Modern technology ironically has exacerbated the stressors inherent in this stage because combatants who have cellular phones and other electronic devices are able to communicate their distress to their families. The unfortunate result is the high probability of secondary traumatization of significant others. The main challenges of the non-deployed parent are to maintain the new family routines and secure additional financial or emotional support for the family.

The next stage in the process is re-deployment. Re-deployment is the service member's homecoming. The homecoming and reunification process, also have several stages that do not all occur at once. Mateczun and Holmes (1996) describe homecoming as a process of reunion or repatriation that has three components: return, readjustment, and reintegration. The return is the first stage of the reunion process and is the physical reunion of those who have been separated (Mateczun & Holmes, 1996).

Although the return is a joyous event it may also be a very stressful event because of the associated uncertainty (Kennedy, 2004; Mateczun & Homes, 1996). Both the veteran and other family members worry about how much the other has changed. Homecoming rituals are extremely important during this stage of reunion because they remind returning veterans that they are no longer at war and remind other family members that it is time for everyone to readjust to life with the veteran at home.

Mateczun and Holmes (1996) describe the second component of their model, readjustment, in somewhat surreal terms. They suggest that it is as if "individuals recognize each other but ... sense that the other is not really who he or she says he or she is" (p. 378). The most common clinical difficulties, e.g., suicidal or homicidal ideation, tend to arise during this period. Fears of betrayal and issues related to loyalty or sexual fidelity become prominent. This is a particularly dangerous period for those who have developed no family support system (Mateczun & Holmes, 1996).

The third component of Mateczun and Holmes' (1996) reunion model is reintegration. Reintegration corresponds to the last phase of the cycle described by Kennedy (2004) as post-deployment. This is the period that occurs after the parties, celebrations, and initial flurry of excitement that accompanies the veteran's homecoming. It is the period of time when both the service member and the family begin to readjust to being together again. This stage is characterized by the effort of all family members to recognize and accept the changes that have occurred in individuals and between family members during the separation and to then create a new family system based on negotiating and integrating responding to these changes and accommodating the "loses of reunion." Some of the roles, thoughts, and behaviors of family members and the veteran acquired during the separation must be set aside in order for the family to function as a healthy unit. The major task for the service member is to accept the changes that have occurred in the family routine and family members during his or her absence and to re-establish his or her relationships with family members. Unfortunately, this is not always easy for the veteran to accomplish, but all individuals must accommodate to the new structure or the structure will fail (Mateczun & Holmes, 1996).

The major challenges for the family are to accept the physical and psychological changes that may have occurred in the service member and to realize that readjustment to family life may be more difficult for the service member than they expected.

Reintegration and readjustment are not synonymous with recovery. The brief period of euphoria that accompanies the return may be quickly replaced by a period of disorientation, confusion, and despair, and there is no guarantee that psychological signs and symptoms of distress will subside without intervention. Accordingly, in order for a homecoming to really be successful it will be probably be appropriate to build upon the Mateczun & Holmes (1996) model and add the additional stage of recovery. Recovery would probably take a few weeks to a few months to accomplish. This stage would be characterized by harmonious interaction of the veteran with civilian friends and family members and co-workers in the work environment as well. The veteran will have adjusted to his new civilian status and integrated both his military and civilian worldviews in a meaningful way. The veteran may still have unpleasant memories concerning his or her war zone experiences, but these feelings and thoughts will not dominate the veteran's life.

Indicators of Problematic Readjustment for Families

Wilson and Wilson (1985), state that marital support and healthy family dynamics are crucial factors in the successful readjustment of combat veterans. Unfortunately, not all families are healthy. Family conflict can result in increased stress within the family which can trigger PTSD symptoms; high levels of emotion can also impede the veteran's improvement (Sherman, Zanotti, & Jones, 2005). Wilson and Wilson suggest that six behaviors tend to characterize dysfunctional veteran families. These are:

(a) viewing the veteran as the identified patient,

(b) living in isolation and avoiding intimacy,

(c) having financial instability due to substance abuse,

(d) using hurtful language and rage,

(e) presenting inappropriate responses to loss, and

(f) having "unspoken rules"

Having the veteran occupy the identified patient role makes him or her, the exclusive source of difficulty in the family. The veteran may be the identified patient, but the problems he or she experiences occur and are perpetuated as a result of his or her interactions with other people (Wilson & Wilson, 1985).

Since family systems operate with their own rituals, roles, and rules of interaction, attempts to restore the health of the veteran may threaten members of the system. There may be great security in being able to blame the veteran for everything that is wrong in the family system. Although many veterans will have adjustment issues, having them serve as scapegoats for the family is clearly not healthy.

Another characteristic of dysfunctional veteran families is that they tend to be socially isolated and alienated. They tend to be socially isolated in deference to the veteran's unease in social situations. Moreover, the families are also internally isolated. Family members avoid intimacy because they fear getting hurt if they allow closeness or vulnerability (Wilson & Wilson, 1985). Also, it is not uncommon for substance abuse, most frequently alcohol, to have a substantial impact on both the financial and emotional stability of the family (Wilson & Wilson). It is likely, as well, that an enabling partner may cover up or make excuses for this behavior.

Violent outbursts, abusive language and physical violence may also occur within the family particularly when substance abuse occurs. Veterans may have difficulty regulating their emotions and their fears of losing control are transformed into rage directed at family members. This inappropriate display of affect also extends to situations involving loss or illness. Instead of showing sympathy when family members are in pain or die, the veteran may becomes hostile and distant, even though the veteran has a strong emotional attachment to the family member. Wilson and Wilson (1985), state that this behavior is actually a display of the emotional numbing that is common to PTSD. Nonetheless, the result of this behavior is that other family members may feel hurt, rejected, and unsupported.

Finally, all of these feelings may be compounded because unhealthy families also tend to have a "no talking" rule about both the veteran's current behavior and the veteran's combat experience. Unfortunately, this rule encourages veterans to repress their memories, keeps them emotionally isolated from their significant others (Wilson & Wilson, 1985), and builds resentment in other family members for the veteran's seemingly failure to live in the present. Wilson and Wilson (1985) state that the primary goals of therapy with veteran families should be to increase cooperation and support between family members and to develop specific interpersonal skills the family may be missing. This may be accomplished by (a) removing the veteran from the identified patient role and establishing shared responsibility and mutual support for creating change, (b) clarifying the values of the family and the roles that the adults occupy, (c) agreeing on rules for the healthy expression of anger, (d) finding a means for the veteran to express painful war experiences, and (e) engaging in skills training to overcome specific deficiencies in the family system (Wilson & Wilson, 1985).

Although these goals were developed to assist Vietnam veteran families, they still remain relevant and useful in working with contemporary veteran families.

Evidence for the Inclusion of Families in Therapy

As noted above, it has been found that social support from their families is instrumental in the veteran's recovery from PTSD. The inclusion of family member in treatment increases the likelihood of creating positive, enduring change for the veteran. Furthermore, without helping the veteran's family, it is likely that they will continue to engage in familiar and often dysfunctional patterns (Sherman et al., 2005).

Despite the often adverse effects of PTSD on relationships, couples therapy addressing these issues is scarce (Sherman et al., 2005). Sherman, Zanotti, and Jones (2005), suggest that intervening to help partners of veterans with PTSD manage their stress levels will help them to experience greater relationship satisfaction. This is important for the interpersonal relationships of all parties involved. They propose that in depth couples therapy should draw upon each person's unique strengths, taking into account both parties needs and challenging couples to make positive, sustainable changes. In addition, assisting the veteran in educating their partner about symptoms, teaching their partner to support them during episodes, and teaching the couple to deescalate the situation and promote learning is essential.

Sherman (2003) describes a caregiver program that fulfills many of these needs. The Support and Family Education Program (SAFE), is a fourteen session curriculum that is facilitated by mental health professionals and although is not diagnostic specific includes attention to PTSD. The goals of the SAFE program are to: teach caregivers about symptoms and course of mental illness; give families the opportunity to ask questions of mental health professionals; decrease stigma associated with mental illness; publicize the availability of mental health services; help families to understand the importance of early intervention; and link families to resources. This program was developed and run through a VA hospital and was catered towards veterans and their families. Results found that program attendance was correlated to increased understanding of mental illness, increased awareness of VA programs, and increased levels of participants' self-care. Although the SAFE program is not PTSD specific, such programs can foster interdependent, balanced family relations and be an important element in the comprehensive treatment of PTSD (Sherman et al., 2005).

The Family: A Case Study
Assessment of a Complex Clinical Case and an Initial Treatment Plan

Melody, a 35 year-old Caucasian female came in complaining of feelings of depression over her husband's aloof attitude towards her since his return from Iraq. Melody suspects that her husband, John, who is 28-years old, is having an extramarital affair because he seems distracted and "emotionally detached." She reports that lately he has been drinking excessively and having nightmares in which he wakes up in the middle of the night, screaming and scrambling for his pocket knife that he keeps by his side of the bed. She wonders if he is suffering from combat stress but he denies it and he refuses to talk about the events that occurred while he was deployed in Iraq.

Melody and John have an 8 year-old-son, Michael. Michael's teacher has been complaining to Melody that Michael is hyperactive in school and that he is not completing his assignments. Melody feels that his teacher maybe overly critical of Michael and not working with Michael to help him succeed in school. Melody often feels helpless and frustrated over Michael's behaviors. Melody has the primary parenting responsibility as John works long hours and has gone on several tours that have lasted a year or longer since Michael was born.

Melody feels isolated as a housewife and has had trouble making friends. She reported having made a few female friends from her neighborhood, but the "women just like to gossip and spread rumors" and she feels that she cannot trust them, in fact, she feels as though she can't trust anyone.

(Continued)

Melody's family of origin lives out of state and although she reaches out to them for support, they are often unable to offer her emotional support because of their own issues with alcoholism.

Melody came to the first session with the idea that she could bring her husband for conjoint private therapy, as he refuses to see a physician or a counselor on the military base. John does not feel that he has "a problem." He views needing help as a sign of "weakness" and he does not want his commanding officer to think any less of him. He also fears losing his rank and status with the military. At Melody's request, John agreed to attend a therapy session with her.

The assessment of the case begins with the client. In this scenario, Melody is the first one that presents for counseling and it is uncertain if her husband John will be joining her. Thus, the assessment would begin with Melody. Her symptoms of depression need to be further explored and any risk factors associated with a mood disorder (such as suicide ideation) need to be investigated. A psychiatric evaluation for medication may need to be part of the evaluation as well, depending on the severity of her depression and how her depressive symptoms impact her ability to function. Melody's mental health history, medical history, substance abuse history and her family's history in these areas also needs to be assessed. History taking is a crucial component of any assessment. In fact, competent treatment will be based on the findings from a thorough assessment.

If John agrees to come in to a counseling session with Melody, he should also be evaluated in these domains and additionally be screened for Post Traumatic Stress Disorder (PTSD) and a possible Substance Abuse Disorder. Depending on the findings from the evaluation, the social worker may recommend that he seek out further individual treatment to address his PTSD symptoms and/or substance abuse.

Whether one is working with an individual or with a couple, relationship/ marital history is an important element to address. Strengths in a relationship can be assessed and as well as periods of crisis or change. Relationship milestones are important to explore as these transitions are often points of stress (i.e., marriage, having children) and discovering how the couple has coped with such normative transitions will render much information on the couple's current functioning and ability to cope under stress. A thorough history of incidents of domestic violence is always in order.

Michael's functioning in school may also be related to what is happening with his father as form of secondary trauma, or as a response to the couple's marital issues. Risk factors, such as the potential for child abuse may also play a role in Michael's behavior. Another possibility for Michael's problems in school may be independent of these environmental factors, and he may suffer from a childhood mental disorder, such as Attention

(Continued)

Deficit Hyperactivity Disorder. Michael would need to be further assessed in his own right by another social worker to explore his developmental, academic, medical, social and family history. However, first and foremost, it is important to consider whether or not this is Michael's response to the stress being experienced in the home as a result of his father's potential PTSD, before any other diagnosis for Michael is reached. A referral to a social worker who specializes in working with children would need to be made by Melody's social worker. If there is a history of academic problems, psycho-educational testing may also be recommended in order to rule out any learning disabilities.

The social worker then creates an initial collaborative treatment plan with Melody and John to provide couples counseling with the notion that John would seek out his own individual counseling with another clinician to address his PTSD/ Substance Abuse issues. The resistance towards mental health treatment will need to be addressed with John and a starting point could be that he is encouraged to attend combat stress education groups on military base that are less stigmatizing. However, depending on the severity of the PTSD symptoms, he may require a psychiatric evaluation for possible medication. Additionally, a 12-step and/or alcohol rehabilitation program may be in order. Ideally, Melody would also benefit from her own individual work as well, so that she could deal with possible co-dependency issues stemming from growing up in an alcoholic home. Community support groups or military wives' support groups may also be helpful for Melody to decrease her isolation and begin experimenting with forming some healthy relationships with her peers. Parenting education would also be helpful in providing additional support on how to help Michael and increase Melody's and John's feelings of efficacy in their parenting roles.

Military Issues Self-Assessment
Cycle of Deployment and Re-deployment

Match the letter of the following deployment concepts with the words or statements that follow them.

    A. Pre-deployment
    B. Deployment
    C. Sustainment
    D. Re-deployment
    E. Post-deployment
    F. Recovery

1.   Period during which younger children may regress in social and/or intellectual development   _____

2.   The period during which the war zone stressors take their greatest toll   _____

3.   The service member's homecoming   _____

4.   When service members and their families experience the greatest physical and emotional separation   _____

5.   Period during which new family roles and responsibilities are established   _____

6.   When the most common clinical difficulties for veterans tend to arise   _____

7.   The period characterized by the effort of all family members to recognize and accept the changes that may have occurred in service members and the family system   _____

8.   The period after the celebrations and excitement of the veteran's homecoming   _____

9.   Period during which fears of betrayal and issues related to loyalty and sexual fidelity typically arise   _____

10.   Period during which older children may begin to act-out and challenge boundaries as a coping mechanism   _____

11.   Period during which the likelihood of suicide is highest   _____

12. Period of social withdrawal between service members and their families _____

13. Typical period of greatest challenge for the non-deployed parent or caregiver. _____

14. Reintegration is the major theme of this phase _____

15. Period during which veterans are most likely to consider reenlistment _____

16. The period that begins when service members receive orders to deploy _____

17. Typical period of greatest financial hardship for non-deployed parent or caregiver _____

18. Period during which service members develop their daily war zone routines _____

19. Period during which service members are most likely to manifest PTSD-like symptoms _____

20. Reunion is the major theme of this phase _____

21. Period characterized by harmonious interactions of veteran with family members, civilian friends, and co-workers _____

Answers: Cycle of Deployment and Re-Deployment

20. d	15. d	10. b	5. b
19. d	14. e	9. d	4. c
18. c	13. c	8. d	3. d
17. c	12. a, d	7. e	2. c
21. f	16. a	11. d	6. d	1. b

Glossary of Military Related Terms

The following glossary of military related terms includes words and phrases that service members may (or may not use) while describing their experiences in the military. The list is presented in alphabetical order and is intended to be informative but not exhaustive. New terms are created often from military personnel and from government sources so it is beyond the scope of this primer to include all of them. Some of the terms and phrases included here are associated with a particular war or time period, while others are not. Those that are associated with a particular timeframe will include that designation. A substantial number of the terms and phrases are associated with the Vietnam Era. A larger proportion of terms from this era are included in the glossary. Much of the language of these veterans no longer has contemporary contextual meaning so although some words may sound the same, their meaning may have been different in the 1970s.

81 Mike-Mike   81 millimeter mortar

A-10   A twin-engine subsonic turbofan tactical fighter bomber; fires a variety of surface-to-air weapons in a close air support role; also known as the "tank buster."

Abaya   Term for the full body cloak worn by women in Saudi Arabia and other Muslim countries.

Abeam   The transfer of personnel and/or supplies by rigs between two or Replenishment more ships moving side by side while at sea.

Abort	To terminate a mission for any reason other than enemy action.
ACOG	Advanced Combat Optical Gun-sight; low power, very rugged rifle scope
Active duty	Continuous duty on a daily basis; comparable to the civil term "full-time employment"
AD	Accidental discharge of a weapon (This is a serious military offense).
Agent Orange	An herbicide and defoliant containing dioxin, a potent carcinogen sprayed from airplanes in order to clear extensive areas of vegetation in Vietnam that provided cover for enemy troops.
Airborne	Troops trained primarily to effect an assault debarkation especially by parachuting to the site.
AK	Kalishnikov-designed assault rifle used by Russian and Chinese Soldiers (also known as an AK-47)
Al-Jazeera	Middle Eastern television station operating uncensored twenty- four hours each day from Qatar.
Al-Jihad	Militant group of Islamic extremists also known as the Egyptian Islamic Jihad. This group was blamed for the assassination of Egyptian President Anwar Sadat in 1995 in response for his attempts to make peace with Israel. Al-Jihad leaders later joined forces with Osama bin Laden to create Al-Qaeda.
Al Qaeda	The multinational militant Islamic organization headed by Osama bin Laden responsible for the 9/11 attacks in the U.S. Current Al Qaeda members are primarily from Egypt and Saudi Arabia but other Arab and Muslim countries are represented in the membership.
Ao-Dai (oh-die)	Long traditional Vietnamese women's dress
AO	Area of Operations or Aerial Observer
APC	Armored personnel carrier

Arc-light	B-52 bomber air strike (also, "rolling thunder")
Article 5, NATO	The clause in the charter of the North American Treaty Organization that states that in the case of an attack on a member nation, other members will treat the attack as an attack upon themselves. It was invoked for the first time after the 9/11 attacks.
Army	The largest unit in the organizational chain of command. An "Army" is comprised of 50,000 + soldiers under the command of a lieutenant general or higher officer. Army groups have not been employed since WWII; also one of the major service branches.
ARTY	Artillery
ARVN	(ar-vin) Army of the Republic of South Vietnam, a South Vietnamese Soldier
AT-4	Replacement for the M-72 LAAW; much bigger and more Powerful weapon
Auto Get'em	Automatic weapons fire set to "fully auto"(also, "rock and roll")
Axis of Evil	Term used by President George W. Bush during the 2002 State of the Union address to describe "rouge" nations possessing or actively seeking to acquire weapons of mass destruction; specific references were made to North Korea, Iraq and Iran.
Ayatollah	Title meaning "miraculous sign of Allah" used to describe high status Shia (Islamic) scholars
B-52	Very large long-range jet propelled bomber capable of intercontinental flight, also large marijuana cigarette(Vietnam Era)
Battalion	A unit of from 300 to 1,000 soldiers under the command of a lieutenant colonel.
Baby-San	Vietnamese child

Balkans, The	Eastern European countries that lie between the Black Sea and the Adriatic Sea. They also include countries that were part of the former Yugoslavia as well as countries that were part of the former Soviet Union. These countries include: Albania, Bosnia-Herezegovinia, Bulgaria, Croatia, Greece, Macedonia, Moldova, Montenegro, Romania, and Serbia (including the autonomous region of Kosovo).
Beanies	Special Forces personnel (Vietnam era)
Bear hunting with a switch	Undermanned, lightly armed, reconnaissance patrol
Beaucoup (boo-koo)	Many or big (Vietnamese slang)
Beef and Rocks	Beef and potatoes
Beehive	Anti-personnel flachette round
Bird-Shit	Paratroopers or Scrambled Eggs (Vietnam era)
Blue Line	Stream or river as depicted on military maps
Body Count	Number of enemy dead, used to determine the success of a mission
Boom-boom Girl	Whore (Vietnam Era)
Boonies	Jungle or in the field (also Bush)
Bouncing Betty	A land mind which propels itself upward and explodes at waist- level when triggered.
Brigade	A unit of from 3,000-5,000 soldiers under the command of a colonel.
Bringing Smoke	Out- going artillery fire
Bronco (OV-10)	Small twin propeller airplane (Vietnam-Era)
Burka	A full body cloak or veil worn by women in the Middle East having only a space or the woman's eyes. This garment was mandated by the Taliban in Afghanistan.

Butt-Fucked   Attacked from the rear

Butter-Bar   Second Lieutenant (also known as Goonie-Looie)

C-4   Composition-4, a highly destructive plastic high explosive substance

CA   Combat Assault

C & C   Command and Control Helicopter

CAP Team   Combined action platoon

Can of Worms   Spaghetti

Care Package   A package sent from home containing food and/or personal items.

'C' Grease   C-rations

Chain of Command   The succession of commanding officers from a superior to a subordinate through which command is executed; also the following organizational structure of a branch of the armed forces: squad, platoon, company, battalion, brigade, division, corps, and army.

Chairborne Rangers   Clerks (Vietnam Era)

Charlie   Term for Viet Cong soldiers; also VC, Victor Charlie, and Sir Charles (Vietnam Era)

Cartridge Trap   Booby trap using live round set to discharge when stepped on

Cherry Juice   Hydraulic fluid

Chi-com   Chinese Communist

Chieu Hoi (chew-loi)   Surrendered or defected enemy soldier (Vietnam-Era)

Chinook   CH-47 Helicopter (also, Shit-hook)

Claymore   Anti-personnel mine

Click   Kilometer

Cluster Fuck	Anything that is disorganized; also grunts that gather in small groups
Clyde	Enemy troops (Vietnam-Era)
CO	Commanding Officer; also Conscientious Objector
Cocksuckers	Leeches (Vietnam-Era)
Cold LZ	Landing zone not under enemy fire
Collateral damage	Unintended or accidental injury or damage to persons or objects that would not be lawful military targets in the circumstances ruling at that time. Such damage is not considered to be unlawful as long as it is not excessive in light of the overall military advantage anticipated from the attack.
Company	A unit of from 62 to 190 soldiers led by a captain.
Contact	Action with the enemy force
Corps	The Marine Corps; also a unit of 20,000 to 45,000 soldiers under the command of a lieutenant general.
CP	Command post
Crispy Critters	Burned bodies, usually resulting from a Napalm strike
Crotch	Self-depreciating or derogatory term for the Marine Corps (also Jar Heads)
CUNT	Civilian Under Naval Training
Dai-uy (dai-wee)	Captain (Vietnamese)
Delta Tango	Defensive Target. (also, DT)
Daisy Cutter	A 15, 000 pound bomb designed to clear landing zones.
Depleted Uranium	The name for the element U-238 used to make very dense armor-piercing munitions. These munitions are controversial because they leave ground water and air radioactive and have reportedly been linked to increased rates of cancer among the children of soldiers who used DU munitions. The US Department of Defense denies that this is a health risk.

Deployment	To systematically station military persons or forces over an area or the movement of forces within an area of military operation; also the positioning of forces into a formation for battle. The term refers to military personnel being on temporary assignment away for their home base over an extended period of time.
Desert Storm	Name for the 1991 Gulf War that resulted when Iraq invaded Kuwait.
DEROS	Date of Expected Return from Overseas (Vietnam Era).
Deuce and a half	Two and one half-ton truck
Di di	Fast or quick (Vietnamese)
Dien Cai Dau	Vietnamese term for "crazy" or "mentally disturbed." (dinky-dow)
Ditty Bag	Shower kit, or "do-it-yourself" bag for short duration move.
Division	A unit of 10,000-15,000 soldiers under the command of a major general.
Djellaba	Term for the flowing gown worn by men in Saudi Arabia and other Muslim countries.
"Doc", Squid	Any sailor; especially a medic (Vietnam Era)
Donut Dollies	Civilian women volunteers from the Red Cross who served coffee and donuts
Drag	Rear Security
Dump, the	Mortuary
Dung-lai	To stop or halt
Dust-Off	Medical evacuation helicopter or that mission (also Med-Evac and Buzz-Off)
DUSTWUN	"Duty status-whereabouts unknown". A transitory casualty status used when a military commander suspects that a service member may be a casualty but lacks sufficient evidence to make a determination of missing or killed.

DZ   Drop zone

E&E   "Escape and Evasion", avoiding a hazardous assignment

Eagle flight   Large unite helicopter combat assault

El Cid   US Central Intelligence Division or a generic term for spies.

FAC   Forward Air Controller

Family Advocacy   A military social service program that focuses on prevention,

Program (FAP)   Identification and treatment of spouse abuse as well as child abuse and neglect. Generally, military family advocacy programs provide families with direct services and they conduct various prevention, training, and data-collection activities.

Fedayeen   Arabic term or guerilla fighters; applied especially to anti-Israeli Palestinian groups such as Hamas and the PLO.

Firefight   Violent battle of short duration

Fire Mission   Artillery or mortar fire

Flakey   Term describing a bad soldier; one making mistakes

Flying Lesson   Disposing of prisoners by throwing them out of a helicopter

FNG   Fuckin' New Guy

FO   Forward Observer (artillery spotter)

Four Deuce   4.2-inch mortar

Frag   Fragmentation ammunition, especially hand grenades.

Fragging   Personal attacks on military personnel, especially officers, by other military personnel with hand grenades.

Friendlies   Term used to describe allied or American units or soldiers.

Frisbees Crackers (Vietnam Era)

Fruit Salad Military award ribbons worn on the uniform of military personnel.

FTA Fuck the Army

Fucked up To be troubled or seriously wounded

Gimp Incompetent grunt and/or poor soldier (also, Non-hacker)

Golf ball and Meatballs and beans (Vietnam Era) Bullets

Genocide Intentional attempted annihilation of a specific ethnic group.

Gone on a Walk 30-day contact patrol (Vietnam Era)

Gook Derogatory term for any North Vietnamese or Viet Cong soldier (also Slope, Dink, Zip, and Zipper Head).

Gook Sore Any skin sore or infection (also called "crud"

Grease Rations or "to kill someone"

Green Authentic American currency

Green Weenie Army commendation medal (also the military in general) (Vietnam era)

Grunt Infantry soldier or Marine

Gulf War Syndrome A constellation of debilitating symptoms of unknown etiology experienced by veterans of the Person Gulf conflict that includes headaches, muscular and joint pains, memory loss, agitation, and personality change.

Gunship Heavily armed helicopter (also Cobra gunship)

Gun run Path aircraft take when expending ordnance

Hamas Islamic resistance movement dedicated to the total destruction of Israel

Ham and Mother Ham and lima beans (Vietnam Era). Fuckers

Ham and Son-of-	Ham and eggs (Vietnam Era) A-Bitches
Hardshell	A transferred soldier
Head	Drug user (Vietnam-Era) (also, Smacker and Popper).
Heat Tabs	Fuel tablets used to heat water and rations.
Hezbollah (Hizbolla)	An anti-Israeli resistance group comprised of Lebanese Shiites. This group operates T.V. and radio stations as well as health care clinics, and also holds seats in the Lebanese parliament.
Ho Chi Mhins	Rubber sandals made form tire carcasses (Vietnam-Era)
Honcho	Leader or boss
Hootch	Residence, including tent or other temporary shelter (Vietnam-Era)
Hot Lz	Landing zone under enemy fire
Huey	Standard Bell helicopter
Hump	To walk or carry
I&I	Intoxication and Intercourse
Inactive Reserve	Affiliation with the military in a non-training, non-paying status after completing the Duty minimum obligation of active duty service.
In-coming	Received enemy fire, especially artillery
IED	Improvised explosive device
Infantry	Units of the military that are trained, armed, and equipped to fight on foot.
Insurgency	An armed rebellion by any irregular armed force that rises up against an established authority or government.
Intifada	Arabic term for "uprising"; typically refers to Palestinian insurrections against Israel.

"J"	Marijuana cigarette (also, Joint) (Vietnam Era).
Jihad	Arabic word meaning "struggles" and referring to Muslims' individual attempts to improve themselves and grow closer to Allah. The contemporary meaning, however, refers to 'holy war" between Muslims and non-Muslims. Although "holy war" is one meaning of jihad, the tactics of Al Qaeda do not warrant the term jihad. The tenants of Islam forbids harming non-combatants (such as women and children) and also forbids taking one's own life as in the case of so-called suicide bombers.
Jody	Civilian men (Vietnam Era).
John Wayne'n	Displaying reckless heroic behavior in combat.
Jolly Green Giant	Large cargo helicopter (Vietnam Era).
Joy Pop	Flying fast and close to the ground in a helicopter (Vietnam-Era).
Khalifa	Term for the head scarf worn by men in Saudi Arabia and other Muslim countries.
KIA	Killed in Action
Killing zone	An area in which a commander plans to force the enemy to concentrate so as to be destroyed with conventional weapons or the tactical employment of nuclear weapons.
Kurds	Ethnically distinct non-Arab inhabitants of northern Iraq and parts of Turkey. Thousands of Kurds were massacred by the Iraqi army when they were encouraged to rebel against Saddam Hussein in 1991 by the U.S but the U.S. failed to support them militarily.
LAAW	Light anti-tank assault weapon operated by one soldier
Land of the big PX	Reference to the US (Vietnam Era).
LBJ	Long Bing Jail (Vietnam Era).
LEG	Non-airborne soldier, an infantryman.

LGH	Large green helicopter
Lifer	Career military personnel
LOH	Light Observation Helicopter (also LOACH)
"Lonely Eagles"	Name for African American fighter pilots during WWII
Long Rats	Dehydrated rations used by L.R.R.P.'s
L.R.R.P.	Long Range Reconnaissance Patrol
M-240G	Replacement for the M-60 series of infantry and aircraft mounted machine guns
M-249	Squad Automatic Weapon; a light machine gun carried by selected infantrymen
Mad Minute	A 60-second expenditure of ordnance, heavy defensive fire.
Mama-San	Vietnamese woman
MEPS	Military Entrance Processing Station. Military bases at various locations in the U.S. that receive and train new enlisted personnel.
MGH	Medium green helicopter
MIA	Missing in Action
Mk-19	A 40mm belt-fed grenade launcher
Mk-153	SMAW (Shoulder Launched Multipurpose Assault Weapon)
Mog, The	Mogadishu, Somalia
MOS	Military occupational specialty.
MP	Military Police officer

MPC   Military Pay Certificate (also, Script)

MRE   Meals Ready to Eat; Military field rations.

Mujahideen   Arabic word meaning " holy warrior'. This term is applied especially to the Muslims (moo.ha.deen)   who came to Afghanistan in the 1980s to fight against the Soviet forces in Afghanistan.

Muy Huy Duc   "Kiss my ass."(Vietnamese) (me-hoy.duck)

NATO   North Atlantic Treaty Organization. This military alliance was originally created in 1949 to oppose the threat of the Soviet Union's further spread of communism into Western Europe. The original member nations pledged mutual military support in the advent of an attack on any member nation. Since the collapse of the Soviet Union in 1991, there has been some question about the continuing purpose of NATO. Current members of NATO include: Belgium, Canada, the Czech Republic, Denmark, France, Germany, Greece, Hungary, Iceland, Italy, Luxembourg, the Netherlands, Norway, Poland, Portugal, Spain, Turkey, the U.S. and the U.K. Ironically, Russia is also now a member of NATO.

NCO   Non-Commissioned Officer; an enlisted person in pay grade E-4 or higher.

NDP   Night defense position

New Puppy   Ensign; 2nd Lt.

Ngyeun (n-win)   Enemy soldier (Vietnamese)

Nouc (nook)   Water

Nuoc Mam   Fermented fish sauce

Number –One   The best or first (Vietnam-Era)

Number –Ten   The worst or last (Vietnam-Era)

NVA   North Vietnamese Army(also, PAVN)

Obligation	The period of time an individual agrees to serve on active duty, in the reserves, or a combination of both.
OCS	Officer Candidate School. A program for college graduates with no prior military training that wish to become military officers. The program also accepts qualified enlisted personnel who wish to become officers; also, "On Civilian Streets."
Off	To kill someone (Vietnam era)
Ong Biet (comm-bic)	"I don't understand" (Vietnamese)
OPEC	Organization of Petroleum Exporting Countries. A cartel formed by Saudi Arabia, Iran, Iraq, Kuwait and Venezuela in 1960 to control the world's petroleum prices. Current members also include Algeria, Gabon, Indonesia, Libya, Nigeria, Qatar, and the United Arab Emirates.
OPCON	Operational control
Osama bin Laden	Militant Islamic millionaire known primarily as the founder and leader of Al Qaeda and the mastermind of the 9/11 attacks in New York and Washington, D.C. Now viewed as a villain, bin Laden was actually held in high regard by the U.S. and Saudi Arabia for his part in training and leading the mujahideen against the Soviet forces fighting in Afghanistan in the 1980s. Bin Laden's anger with the U.S. began in the 1990s and persists to the present due, in part, to the military presence of the U.S. in Saudi Arabia, the economic sanctions against Iraq, and the seemingly unconditional support of the U.S. for Israel.
Out-going	Friendly fire, especially artillery, directed toward the enemy.
Oversexed Weekly	Newspaper (Vietnam-Era)
P's	Piasters. Vietnamese currency
Papa-San	Vietnamese male adult
Paste	Peanut butter (Vietnam Era)

Pay Grade	Newcomers, without previous military experience and without a college education, normally entering the military as recruits in pay grade E-1. The enlisted pay grades range form E-1 through E-9 with increasing responsibility and salary as the pay grade increases. Officer pay grades rang from O-1 through O-9.
Pecker-Checker	Medic
PFC	Private First Class or Proud Fucking Civilian
Play Dough	Bread (Vietnam-Era)
Point man	First soldier in a column or on patrol
Potato Masher	Chinese communist hand grenade
PRC-25 or-77	Portable radio communication model 25 or model 77(also, Prick)
PRU	Provincial reconnaissance unit
PSYOPS	Psychological operations
Punji Sticks	Sharpened bamboo stakes used as bobby traps
QCS	Vietnamese military police
Quad-50	Four .50 caliber machine guns mounted together as one unit
Ranger	Rapidly deployable airborne light infantry armed and trained to conduct highly complex joint direct actions in coordination with or in support of other special operations units of all service branches.
RCH	Red Cunt Hair (one-half kilometer)
RECON	Reconnaissance. A mission undertaken to obtain information about the activities and resources of an enemy or potential enemy or to secure data concerning the metrological, hydrographic, or geographic characteristics of a particular area.

Redleg	Artillery
Red Ball Express	Army Service and Supply unit in Europe composed primarily of African American truckers during WWII
R.E.M.F.	Rear Echelon Mother Fucker (Vietnam Era)
Remington Raiders	Clerks; also called Smith-Corona Raiders
Reserves	The military forces comprised of individuals who are not presently on full-time active duty but who may be called to active duty if needed.
RF/PF, Ruff-Puffs	Regional or popular forces
Roach Coach	Mobile Mess (food serving) Vehicle
Rocket City	Da Nang (in Vietnam)
Rocket Pocket	Location from which the enemy fires (especially 122mm) rockets.
ROE	Rules of Engagement. Directives issued by military authority that delineate the circumstances and limitations under which U.S. forces will initiate and /or continue combat engagement with other forces encountered (a.k.a, Law of War).
Rogue State	Term first used during the Clinton administration to describe those countries believed to sponsor terrorism. The current list includes Cuba, Iraq, Iran, Libya, North Korea, Sudan, and Syria.
ROK	Republic of Korea (South Korea); also a Marine from that country.
ROK Rats	Korean "C" rations (Vietnam-Era)
ROTC	Reserve Officer's Training Corps. Refers to a program on college campuses designed to train undergraduate students who wish to become officers in the military upon graduation. Incentives for participation in the program include scholarships for tuition, books, and fees; uniforms; and a monthly allowance.

Root, The   Beirut, Lebanon. Term used by service members assigned peacekeeping duty in the 1983 time frame

RPG   Rocket Propelled Grenade

R&R   Rest and Relaxation

RPG   Soviet-style, rocket propelled grenade-launcher

RTC   Radio telephone communicator

Saigon Tea   Orange sodas or cold tea drank by bar girls (Vietnam-Era)

Sea Duty   An assignment (generally for three years) to any ship whether or not scheduled for deployment, or to any aircraft squadron that may or may not be deployable; the term typically refers to Navy personnel.

SGH   Small green helicopter

Shah   Title used to describe high status leaders in Iran

Shariah   Term meaning "the path that leads to God" and refering to Islamic law. Shariah law is based on the Koran, the sunna (other writings of Muhammad) and the hadith (outside observations of Muhammad's life). Strict interpretations of Shariah have resulted in amputations and beheadings for violations of the law.

Shiite   Those who follow the Shia branch of Islam; Shiites believe that the only legitimate leaders of Islam must be blood relatives of the prophet Muhammad. Most Arabs are Sunni Muslims and relations between Sunnis and Shiites are poor.

Shore Duty   All duty performed within the 48 contiguous states where Navy personnel are reassigned to land-based activities and commands. Navy personnel assigned to shore duty are not required to be absent from the corporate limits of the duty station for more than 99 days per year.

Short   Having less than three months left in Vietnam, (also Short-timer)

Shrine   Latrine (also, shitter)

Sit Rep	Situation Report
"SIX", "6"	Commander's radio call-sign
Six-By, 6 BY 6	Military truck with 6-wheel drive
"Skinny"	Enemy combatant during the conflict in Somalia; also "Skines".
Sky Pilot	Chaplain
Slick	UH-1 helicopter, generic term for helicopter (also, Huey. Chopper, or Bird)
Sneaky Petes	Special Forces personnel (Vietnam Era)
Soul Brother	African American soldier or Marine (Vietnam–Era)
Souvenir	To give without cost (Vietnam-Era)
Spooky and Puff	C-47 aircraft armed with flares and several chain guns the Magic Dragon
Stand down	A three-day rest period for units coming out of the field; also used to describe an occasion when VA and civilian medical personnel provide health care services for homeless veterans in the U.S.
Steam and Clean	Steam bath and massage parlors
Stiffs	Dead bodies
Sunni	The largest branch of Islam. Unlike the Shiities; this branch does not require that religious leaders have to be blood descendants of the prophet Muhammad.
Super-Chicken	Army military rank, Spec 5 or over.
Super-Striper	Army military rank, E-6 or over.
SWAG	Scientific, wild-ass guess

"There it is"   Expression used by grunts to agree or confirm (Vietnam-Era)

Thieu-Uy (to-wee)   Second Lieutenant (Vietnamese)

Titi (tee-tee)   Small or little (Vietnamese slang)

Toe Popper   Small plastic land mine

Toi-le bac-si   "I'm a doctor."(Vietnamese) (toe-lee-bac-ci)

Top Dog   First Sergeant, Master Sergeant (also, Top Kick , and First Shirt)

Torch   To set on fire

Tour of Duty   A specified period of service obligation; also used to describe the location of a duty tour, e.g. "Mediterranean tour of duty."

Track   Tracked vehicle

Trade School   One of the military academies, e.g, West Point, or Annapolis

Travel Bureau   Graves registration (Vietnam-Era)

Triple Nickels, The   The 555th Parachute Infantry Company; the first all African American Paratrooper
companies in the U.S. military formed during WWII

Tunnel Rat   Soldiers or small stature used to enter and clear enemy tunnels

Turtle   Replacement

Unit One Kit   Medical bad use by corpsmen or medics

Vill   Village or Hamlet (Vietnam-Era)

Wasted   To be killed (also, Zapped, Greased, Stitched, Blown Away Bought the Farm, and Ruined His Whole Day)

Weapons of Mass   Term used to describe nuclear, chemical and/or biological weapons possessed by
Destruction   enemy states.

White Mice   Saigon Police (Vietnam-Era)

Willy Pete, WP   White phosphorous; also called "Wilson Pickett."

WIA   Wounded in Action

World, In the   Referring to the United States of America

Xin Loi (sin-loy)   "Sorry about that."

Yards   Indigenous tribal people of Vietnam; Hmong

Zippo Squad   A squad that is designated to burn a village (Vietnam Era)

ZOT   Loser, zero, nothing

Military Organizations

Veterans' Organizations

There are well over two hundred different organizations in the United States that are devoted to veterans' affairs. Some of these groups sponsor particular branches of the armed forces, while others serve all veterans from all eras. The following list of veterans organizations are national in scope, and represent a variety of the types of veterans' service organizations that currently exists. The list is not intended to be exhaustive because new organizations are formed routinely to meet specific or emerging needs.

The organizations that have been highlighted on this list are discussed briefly at the end of this section. Readers are encouraged to discover the veterans' organizations that are active in their local areas as well.

Veteran Organizations Chartered by Congress and Recognized by the Veterans Administration for Claim Representation under laws administered by the Department of Veterans Affairs.

American Ex-Prisoners of War

The American Legion *

American Red Cross

American Veterans of WWII, Korea and Vietnam (AMVETS)

Army & Navy Union, USA, Inc.

Blinded Veterans Association

Catholic War Veterans, USA, Inc.*

Congressional Medal of Honor Society of the USA

Disabled American Veterans*

Gold Star Wives of America, Inc.

Jewish War Veterans of the USA*

Legion of Valor of the USA, Inc.

Marine Corps League

Military Order of the Purple Heart of the USA, Inc .(MOPH)*

Non Commissioned Officers Association (NCOA)*

Paralyzed Veterans of America

Polish Legion of American Veterans, USA

United Spanish War Veterans

Veterans of Foreign Wars of the United States (VFW)*

Veterans of World War I of the USA, Inc

Vietnam Veterans of America, Inc.

Other Veteran Organizations recognized for Claim Representation

American defends of Bataan and Corregidor

American G.I. Forum of the US

American Veterans Committee

Army and Air Force Mutual Aid Association

Fleet Reserve Association

National Amputation Foundations, Inc

Navy Mutual Aid Association

Regular Veterans Association

Seattle Veterans Action Center

Swords to Plowshares: Veterans Rights Organizaton

The Forty and Eight

The Retired Enlisted Association

Vietnam Era Veterans Association of Rhode Island

Other National Organizations that serve Veterans

Air Force Association

Air Force Sergeants Association

Alliance of Women Veterans

Army Gold Star Mothers, Inc.

American Military members Association

American Military Retirees Association

American Veterans for Equal Rights

American War Mothers

Association of Ex-POW of the Korean War, Inc.

Association of the U.S. Army

Blinded American Veterans Foundation

Blue Star Mothers of America, Inc

Brotherhood Rally of All Veterans Organization (BRAVO)

China-Burma-India Veterans Association, Inc

Combined National Veterans Association of America

Destroyer-Escort Sailors Association

Italian American War Veterans Association

Korean War Veterans Association, Inc.

Korean War Veterans Memorial Advisory Board

Military Chaplains Association

Military Justice Clinic, Inc.

Military Order of the World Wars

Military Services Community Network

NAM-POWS, Inc.

National American Military Retirees Association

National Association for Black Veterans, Inc*

National Association for Uniformed Services

National Association of Atomic Veterans

National Association of Concerned Veterans

National Association of Military Widows

National Association of Radiation Survivors

National Association of State Directors of Veterans Affairs

National Association of State Veteran Homes

National Association of Veterans Program Administrators

National Coalition for Homeless Veterans*

National Congress of Puerto Rican Veterans, Inc.

National Gulf War Resource Center, Inc*

National Incarcerated Veterans Network

National League of Families of American Prisoners and Missing in Southeast Asia

National Veterans Legal Services Programs, Inc.*

National Vietnam Veterans Coalition

National World War II Glider Pilots Association

Navy Reserve Association

Navy League of the United States

Ninth Infantry Division Association

OSS-101 Association

Past National Commanders Organization

Pearl Harbor Survivors Association, Inc.

Red River Valley Fighter Pilots Association

Reserve Officers Association of the US

Service Members Legal Defense Network

Society of Military Widows

The Retired Officers Association

Tuskegee Airmen, Inc.

United States Army Warrant Officers Association

U.S. Merchant Marine Veterans of World War II

Veterans of the Vietnam War, Inc.

Veterans United for Strong America

Vietnam Veterans Institute

WAVES National

Women Marines Association

Women Air Force Service Pilots, WWII

Women's Army Corps Veterans Association

In addition, each state and territory in America has an Office of Veterans Affairs.

American Ex-Prisoners of War
http://www.axpow.org/

- The American Ex-Prisoners of War was founded April 14, 1942 by the wives and mothers of soldiers who heard about their sons and husbands who had been taken prisoner. Originally known as the Bataan Relief Organization, their motto was "We will not let them down." This group was very active trying to get relief to the POW's and exchange of information as it came through.

- The purpose of the American Ex-Prisoners of War in their motto: "We exist to help those who cannot help themselves." They exist for the purpose of helping others. The organization of former POW's (military and civilian), their spouses, families and civilian internees help those affected by their capture deal with the trauma through friendship of those who share a common experience.

- Membership is open to all former prisoners of war from any theater in any war and all former civilian internees and to the families of such persons. There are no "associate" members and there are no auxiliaries. Each and every member is entitled to all privileges of membership.

The American Legion
http://www.legion.org/

- Founded in Paris, France at first caucus of the American Expeditionary Force in March 1919

- Congress chartered the American Legion as a patriotic, mutual-help, wartime veterans' organization. It is a community-service organization with approximately 3 million members (men and women), with 15,000 American Legion Posts worldwide. Posts are organized into 55 Departments, one each for the 50 states, the District of Columbia, Puerto Rico, France, Mexico, and the Philippines. The national headquarters is in Indianapolis, Indiana. The national organization has a regular full-time staff of about 300 employees.

- Preamble to the Constitution of The American Legion:

For God and Country

We associate ourselves together for the following purposes:

To uphold and defend the Constitution of the United States of American; to maintain law and order; to foster and perpetuate a one hundred percent Americanism; to preserve the memories and incidents of our associations in the great wars; to inculcate a sense of individual obligation to the community state and nation; to combat the autocracy of both the classes and the masses; to make right the master of might; to promote peace and goodwill on earth; to safeguard and transit to posterity the principles of justice, freedom and democracy; to consecrate and sanctify our comradeship by our devotion to mutual helpfulness.

- Eligible for membership, currently on active duty anywhere in the world, or have served during any eligible war eras, and are a veteran of:

  - World War I   April 6, 1917 – November 11,
    1918

  - World War II   December 7, 1941 – Decem
                                                   ber 31, 1948

  - Korean War   June 25, 1950 – January 31,
                                                   1955

  - Vietnam War   February 28, 1961 to May 7,
                                                   1975

  - Lebanon/Grenada   August 24, 1982 – July 31,
                                                   1984

  - Operation Just Cause – Panama   December 20, 1999 – Janu
                                                   ary 31, 1990

  - Gulf War/ War on Terrorism   August 2, 1990 – Present

Catholic War Veterans of the USA
http://cwv.org/

- In early 1935 Msgr. (then Father) Edward J. Higgins, with permission of his Bishop Ordinary, Most Reverend Thomas E. Molloy of the Diocese of Brooklyn, gathered together some few parishioners from his parish, Church of the Immaculate Conception in New York, who had served in World War I and formed the first Post of the CWV.

- The Objectives of the Catholic War Veterans of the USA states:

  The primary objective of the Catholic War Veterans is to make the entire nation acutely aware of the struggle and needs of many veterans, their widows and children. We, as survivors, have an obligation to our fallen brothers and sisters to inform the people of our country that many veterans and their families need asistance; that these veterans have made sacrifices for their country and deserve to be treated accordingly, with proper respect and support.

  It is also the responsibility of the Catholic War Veterans to help protect, preserve and defend the Constitution of the United States and the laws of our government.

As members of the CWV, we are obligated to cooperate to the fullest extent with all veteran organizations in order to better serve the interests of the men and women who served in each of the wars in which our nation has been involved.

However, we must constantly remember, that as Catholics, we are bound to serve God. We can do this in many ways, such as demonstrating our love and respect to individuals without regard to race, creed, color or national origin.

We must strive to instill in the young people of today a respect for our flag, our national anthem, and for the traditions of our great country.

And finally, we must remember that the family is the basic unit or building block in our society. May we ask the Lord's blessing in providing us with the strength and fortitude to achieve our goals.

- Membership is open to any person who is both an American Citizen and a Veteran of the Armed Forces of the United States as herein defined is eligible for membership in the Catholic War Veterans of the United States of America Inc. An applicant shall be a member of the Catholic Church, enlisted, drafted, inducted or commissioned into any branch of the United States Army, Navy, Marine Corps, Coast Guard, Air Force, and/or including the National Guard or Reserve components, and who has served at least 90 days on active duty and who now has a discharge under honorable conditions - and shall include those who have served less than 90 days and are honorably discharged because of a disability incurred in the line of duty or any person currently on active duty or currently serving in the National Guard or Reserves. Also eligible are the U. S. Merchant Marines, provided that such applicant who has served in the Merchant Marines, served at least 90 days between 7 December 1941 to 31 December 1946, including service in the U. S. Army Transport Service or the Naval Transport Service

Disabled American Veterans
http://www.dav.org/

- Formed in 1920 and chartered by Congress in 1932

- Disabled American Veterans (DAV) is the official voice of America's service-connected disabled veterans, representing America's 2.1 million disabled veterans, their families and survivors. The DAV provides nationwide network services free of charge to all veterans and members of their families. The DAV is fully supported by membership dues and contributions from the American public. It is not a government agency, and does not receive any government funding

- Mission Statement:

Made up exclusively of men and women disabled in our nation's defense, the Disabled American Veterans (DAV) is dedicated to one, single purpose: building better lives for all of our nation's disabled veterans and their families. This mission is carried forward by:

☐ Providing free, professional assistance to veterans and their families in obtaining benefits and services earned through military service and provided by the Department of Veterans Affairs (VA) and other agencies of government;

☐ Providing outreach concerning its program services to the American people generally, and to disabled veterans and their families specifically;

☐ Representing the interests of disabled veterans, their families, their widowed spouses and their orphans before Congress, the White House, and the Judicial Branch, as well as state and local government;

☐ Extending the DAV's mission of hope into the communities where these veterans and their families live through a network of state-level Departments and local Chapters; and

☐ Providing a structure through which disabled veterans can express their compassion for their fellow veterans through a variety of volunteer programs.

☐ Membership in the DAV is open to any honorably discharged veteran with a disability incurred in wartime military service or under conditions similar to war.

☐ Any man or woman, who was wounded, gassed, injured or disabled in the line of duty during time of war, while in the service of either the military or naval forces of the United States of America, and who has not been dishonorably discharged or separated from such service, or who may still be in active service in the armed forces of the United States of America is eligible for membership in the Disabled American Veterans. Others who are disabled while serving with any of the armed forces of any nations associated with the United States of America as allies during any of its war periods, who are American citizens and who are honorably discharged, are also eligible.

Jewish War Veterans of the USA
http://www.jwv.org/

- The first meetings of the Jewish War Veterans of the USA was held in March 15, 1896 at the Lexington Opera House in New York City. Sixty-three Jewish Civil War veterans were recorded as present as members of the Hebrew Union Veterans.

- NATIONAL CONSTITUTION

  PREAMBLE

  We, citizens of the United States of America, of the Jewish faith, who served in the Wars of the United States of America, in order that we may be of greater service to our country and to one another, associate ourselves together for the following purposes:

  To maintain true allegiance to the United States of America; to foster and perpetuate true Americanism; to combat whatever tends to impair the efficiency and permanency of our free institutions; to uphold the fair name of the Jew and fight his or her battles wherever unjustly assailed; to encourage the doctrine of universal liberty, equal rights, and full justice to all men and women; to combat the powers of bigotry and darkness wherever originating and whatever their target; to preserve the spirit of comradeship by mutual helpfulness to comrades and their families; to cooperate with and support existing educational institutions and establish educational institutions, and to foster the education of ex-servicemen and ex-servicewomen, and our members in the ideals and principles of Americanism; to instill love of country and flag, and to promote sound minds and bodies in our members and our youth; to preserve the memories and records of patriotic service performed by the men and women of our faith; to honor their memory and shield from neglect the graves of our heroic dead.

- Any person of the Jewish faith of good character, who is a citizen of the United States of America, who was regularly enlisted, drafted, inducted or commissioned, and who was accepted for, and assigned to, active duty in the armed forces of the United States of America (including the National Guard and Reserves), in any of its wars, campaigns, conflicts, or as may be further set forth in the Bylaws; or who being a citizen of the United States of America, at the time of his or her entry therein, served on active duty in the United States of America, during any of the said wars, campaigns, conflicts, or expeditions may be elected to active membership. No person, discharged or released under conditions other than honorable from any such service, shall be eligible to membership.

Election and obligation to active membership shall confer full and equal rights with all other active members of the Jewish War Veterans of the United States of America, without limitation, except as may be provided in the Bylaws, and provided that he or she is in good standing with the National Organization.

Military Order of the Purple Heart
http://www.purpleheart.org/

- The Purple Heart is awarded to members of the armed forces of the U.S. who were wounded by an instrument of war in the hands of the enemy or posthumously to the next of kin in the name of those who are killed in action or die of wounds received in action. It is specifically a combat decoration.

- The Military Order of the Purple Heart was formed in 1932 for the protection and mutual interest of all who have received the decoration. It is composed exclusively of Purple Heart recipients and is the only veterans service organization comprised strictly of "combat" veterans.

- Membership in the Military Order of the Purple Heart is open to persons who have been awarded the Purple Heart Medal By the Government of the United States.

National Association for Black Veterans, Inc.
http://www.nabvets.com/

- Founded in 1969 by seven Vietnam combat veterans, the then known "Interested Veterans of the Central City (IVOCC) incorporated in Milwaukee, Wisconsin, and reorganized in 1973 to become the National Association for Black Veterans (NABVETS). They are a membership service organization whose goal is to address issues concerning Black and other minority veterans.

- The Mission of NABVETS

On an ongoing basis, the National Association for Black Veterans, Inc. will provide strategic advocacy on behalf of its membership with Congress, the Federal Administration, State Administrations and other agencies and organizations. NABVETS will provide personal advocacy on behalf of veterans seeking claims against the United States Department of Veterans Affairs; advocacy for youth in all matters required for successful passage into adulthood; advocacy on behalf of families; with community involvement, provide advocacy in creating positive lifestyles for veterans; and to generate and preserve the historical record.

The Vision of NABVETS

To be a professional organization that has, as its members, 50% of the total black veterans population nationally; an organization with State Departments and Command Councils located in every state and city with a population greater than 250,000; an organization that has an emphasis on younger veterans who are on active duty or who are recently separated veterans; an organization that offers its members a wide array of benefits and services; an organization that provides services to all veterans, but especially low income veterans; and an organization that is financially viable.

National Coalition for Homeless Veterans

http://www.nchv.org/index.cfm

- National Coalition for Homeless Veterans (NCHV) was founded in 1990 by a group of community-based homeless veteran service providers. The NCHV is a nonprofit, tax exempt, 501(c)3 corporation that seeks to eliminate homelessness in the veteran community. NCHV serves as a liaison between branches of the federal government and community-based homeless veteran service providers.

- Mission: NCHV will end homelessness among veterans by shaping public policy, educating the public, and building the capacity of service providers.

- Help for homeless veterans can be accessed at:

    http://www.nchv.org/veteran.cfm

National Gulf War Resource Center, Inc.

http://www.ngwrc.org/index.cfm

- The National Gulf War Resource Center (NGWRC) was founded in 1995 and based at the office of the Vietnam Veterans of America in Washington, DC.

- Mission Statement: The National Gulf War Resource Center is an international coalition of advocates and organizations providing a resource for information, support, and referrals for all those concerned with the complexities of Persian Gulf War issues, especially Gulf War illnesses and those held prisoner or missing in action.

National Veterans Legal Services Program, Inc.

http://www.nvlsp.org/

- The National Veterans Legal Services Program (NVLSP) is an independent, non-profit veterans service organization that has been assisting veterans and their advocates for more than 25 years. NVLSP achieves its mission through education, advocacy, litigation, training advocates who represent veterans, and publications.

- Beginning in the 1980s, NVLSP channeled its efforts to help disabled veterans who had applied to the Department of Veterans Affairs (VA) for disability compensation and health care, but whose claims had been unfairly denied.

- NVLSP has been in the forefront of creating a safety net for veterans who have been unable to secure an advocate by recruiting, training, and publishing advocacy materials for thousands of volunteer attorneys and lay advocates who represent veterans, for free, before the Court and the VA.

Non Commissioned Officers Association
http://www.ncoausa.org/

- NCOA was established in 1960 to enhance and maintain the quality of life for noncommissioned and petty officers in all branches of the Armed Forces, National Guard and Reserves.

- NCOA is committed to those who serve, or have served, to insure that this Nation honors its commitment to provide health care and special benefits for the individual sacrifices of its sons and daughters and maintains with dignity and honor that promise expressed by President Lincoln: ...to care for him who shall have borne the battle and for his widow and his orphan...

The Retired Enlisted Association
http://www.trea.org/

- The Retired Enlisted Association was formed on February 18, 1963 by M/Sgt George Skonce and Retired M/Sgt Dean Sorell, along with other retired enlisted personnel at Ent Air Force Base NCO Club in Colorado Springs, Colorado.

- Mission Statement: To enhance the quality of life for uniformed services enlisted personnel, their families and survivors- including active components and all retirees; to stop the erosion of earned benefits through our legislative efforts, to maintain our esprit de corps, dedication and patriotism, and to continue our devotion and allegiance to God and Country.

- Membership categories:

Regular Members - Any enlisted person, retired from an active or reserve component of the Armed Forces, either for length of service or permanent medical disability shall be eligible for regular membership. A retired member advanced to commissioned or Warrent Officer status, either through recall to active duty or on the retired list shall remain eligible for regular membership as long as his/her dues are kept current. Active duty, Reserve and National Guard enlisted personnel with 10 or more years retirement creditable service shall also be eligible, but membership (including life membership) shall be withdrawn if the person fails to retire from the Armed Forces. The term "regular member" encompasses both charter and life members of TREA.

Associate Members - Widows/widowers of members and non-members, who were eligible for membership at the time of their death, are eligible to join The Retired Enlisted Association as associate members. Associate members are not eligible for life membership. Associate members shall enjoy the privileges of regular membership, except the right to make motions, vote, or hold office.

Veterans for America
http://www.ewol.com/VFA/

- Veterans for America was created from the Veterans Outreach and Assistance Program created by the Vietnam Veterans Chapter 665 in Port Charlotte, FL in 1996.

- The primary thrusts of VFA efforts are to:

    A. Render outreach and assistance to all veterans needing help, and to those in the community when local VFA determines it to be in the best interest of the public good.

    B. Assist the Veterans Administration (VA) in providing authorized, timely, respectful, dignified, competent, and customer (veteran) oriented total quality service to all veterans. (The goal here is that veterans will be satisfied by the efforts of the VA.)

- Coordinating instructions:

    A. The VFA will use all means possible to accomplish its mission: consistent with the best interests of the nation and the rule of law.

    B. All VFA work is strictly voluntary, or as contracted by local VFA authorities. There will be no pay or other remuneration for VFA authorities and volunteers.

    C. VFA is primarily action oriented; VFA provides help for people in need as opposed to building memorials and conducting ceremonies.

D.   VFA does not compete with other veterans groups; VFA embraces all veterans groups regardless of service affiliation or time of service. All veterans and their supporters (associates) are welcome.

E.   VFA depends on the availability of a large group of veterans and their supporters in the local area be entered into the VFA data base to be asked for their help if available for service as situations arise. No VFA member or associate is committed to do anything.

Veterans of Foreign Wars of the United States
http://www.vfw.org/

- The beginnings of the Veterans of Foreign Wars of the United States traces back to 1899 when veterans of the Spanish-American War (1898) and the Philippine Insurrection (1899-1902) founded local organizations to secure rights and benefits for their service. At this time many arrived home wounded or sick and there was no medical care or veterans' pension for them. Some of these veterans banded together and formed organizations with what would become known as the Veterans of Foreign Wars of the United States.

- The VFW assists any veteran, or their dependents, obtain federal or state entitlements, assist veterans, or their dependents, seeking disability compensation, assist veterans in discharge upgrades, record corrections, education benefits and pension eligibility. In addition, service officers regularly inspect VA health care facilities and national cemeteries, and employment specialists monitor laws concerning veterans' preference in federal employment.

  The VFW also monitors medical and health issues affecting veterans as well as providing veterans with up-to-date information on diabetes, post-traumatic stress, Agent Orange exposure and Persian Gulf Syndrome. A recent addition to the Washington D.C., office is the Tactical Assessment Center, a 24-hour help line for veterans with questions or concerns about VA entitlements. (1-800-vfw-1899)

- Membership is determined by using the VFW's eligibility listing, which lists campaign periods and authorized service medals, to determine eligibility for membership.

Vietnam Veterans of America
http://www.vva.org/

- The Vietnam Veterans of America was founded in January 1978, by a small group of Vietnam veteran activists in Washington, D.C. They were searching for allies to support the creation of an advocacy organization devoted exclusively to the needs of Vietnam veterans. At the time the VVA was known as the Council of Vietnam Veterans.

- The purpose of Vietnam Veterans of America's national organization, the state councils, and chapters is:

  ▢ To help foster, encourage, and promote the improvement of the condition of the Vietnam veteran.

  ▢ To promote physical and cultural improvement, growth and development, self-respect, self-confidence, and usefulness of Vietnam-era veterans and others.

  ▢ To eliminate discrimination suffered by Vietnam veterans and to develop channels of communications which will assist Vietnam veterans to maximize self-realization and enrichment of their lives and enhance life-fulfillment.

  ▢ To study, on a non-partisan basis, proposed legislation, rules, or regulations introduced in any federal, state, or local legislative or administrative body which may affect the social, economic, educational, or physical welfare of the Vietnam-era veteran or others; and to develop public-policy proposals designed to improve the quality of life of the Vietnam-era veteran and others especially in the areas of employment, education, training, and health.

  ▢ To conduct and publish research, on a non-partisan basis, pertaining to the relationship between Vietnam-era veterans and the American society, the Vietnam War experience, the role of the United States in securing peaceful co-existence for the world community, and other matters which affect the social, economic, educational, or physical welfare of the Vietnam-era veteran or others.

  ▢ To assist disabled and needy war veterans including, but not limited to, Vietnam veterans and their dependents, and the widows and orphans.

- Their founding principle is "Never again shall one generation of veterans abandon another."

- VVA's goals are to promote and support the full range of issues important to Vietnam veterans, to create a new identity for this generation of veterans, and to change public perception of Vietnam veterans.

- VVA holds as its first principle that the organization is measured by deeds and openness as evidence of the core values of justice, integrity, and meaningful achievement.

- Membership is open U.S. armed force veterans who served on active duty (for other than training purposes) in the Republic of Vietnam between February 28, 1961 and May 7, 1975, or in any duty location between August 5, 1964 and May 7, 1975.

PTSD CheckList - Military Version (PCL-M)

Patient's Name: _____

Instruction to patient: Below is a list of problems and complaints that veterans sometimes have in response to stressful military experiences. Please read each one carefully, put an "X" in the box to indicate how much you have been bothered by that problem in the last month.

Weathers, F.W., Huska, J.A., Keane, T.M. PCL-M for DSM-IV. Boston: National Center for PTSD – Behavioral Science Division, 1991.

This is a Government document in the public domain.

No.	Response:	Not at all (1)	A little bit (2)	Moderately (3)	Quite a bit (4)	Extremely (5)
1.	Repeated, disturbing memories, thoughts, or images of a stressful military experience?					
2.	Repeated, disturbing dreams of a stressful military experience?					
3.	Suddenly acting or feeling as if a stressful military experience were happening again (as if you were reliving it)?					

4.	Feeling very upset when something reminded you of a stressful military experience?					
5.	Having physical reactions (e.g., heart pounding, trouble breathing, or sweating) when something reminded you of a stressful military experience?					
6.	Avoid thinking about or t alking about a stressful military experience or avoid having feelings related to it?					
7.	Avoid activities or situations because they remind you of a stressful military experience?					
8.	Trouble remembering important parts of a stressful military experience?					
9.	Loss of interest in things that you used to enjoy?					
10.	Feeling distant or cut off from other people?					
11.	Feeling emotionally numb or being unable to have loving feelings for those close to you?					
12.	Feeling as if your future will somehow be cut short?					
13.	Trouble falling or staying asleep?					
14.	Feeling irritable or having angry outbursts?					
15.	Having difficulty concentrating?					
16.	Being "super alert" or watchful on guard?					
17.	Feeling jumpy or easily startled?					

The Combat Exposure Scale

The Combat Exposure Scale (CES) is a 7-item self-report measure that assesses wartime stressors experienced by combatants. Items are rated on a 5-point frequency (1 = "no" or "never" to 5 = "more than 50 times"), 5-point duration (1 = "never" to 5 = "more than 6 months"), 4-point frequency (1 = "no" to 4 = "more than 12 times") or 4-point degree of loss (1 = "no one" to 4 = "more than 50%") scale. Respondents are asked to respond based on their exposure to various combat situations, such as firing rounds at the enemy and being on dangerous duty. The total CES score (ranging from 0 to 41) is calculated by using a sum of weighted scores, which can be classified into 1 of 5 categories of combat exposure Apranging from "light" to "heavy." The CES was developed to be easily administered and scored and is useful in both research and clinical settings.

CES

Please circle the number above the answer that best describes your experience

(1)   Did you ever go on combat patrols or have other dangerous duty?

1	2	3	4	5
No	1-3X	4-12x	13-50x	51+times

(2)   Were you ever under enemy fire?

1	2	3	4	5
Never	<1 month	1-3 months	4-6 months	7 mos or more

(3) Were you ever surrounded by the enemy?

1	2	3	4	5
No	1-2X	3-12x	13-25x	26+times

(4) What percentage of the soldiers in your unit were killed (KIA), wounded or missing in action (MIA)?

1	2	3	4	5
None	1-25%	26-50%	51-75%	76% or more

(5) How often did you fire rounds at the enemy?

1	2	3	4	5
Never	1-2X	3-12x	13-50X	51 or more

(6) How often did you see someone hit by incoming or outgoing rounds?

1	2	3	4	5
Never	1-2X	3-12x	13-50x	51 or more

(7) How often were you in danger of being injured or killed (i.e., being pinned down, overrun, ambushed, near miss, etc.)?

1	2	3	4	5
Never	1-2X	3-12x	13-50x	51 or more

Keans, T.M.. Fairbank, J.A., Caddell, J.M., Zimering, R.T.. Taylor, K.L. & Mora. CA (1989)

1 = 0-8 Light   2 = 9-16 Light – Moderate   3 = 17- 24 Moderate   4 = 25 32 Moderate – Heavy

5 = 33 – 41 Heavy

SOURCE: http://www.ptsd.va.gov/professional/pages/assessments/assessment-pdf/CES.pdf

Appendix D

Officer Insignia

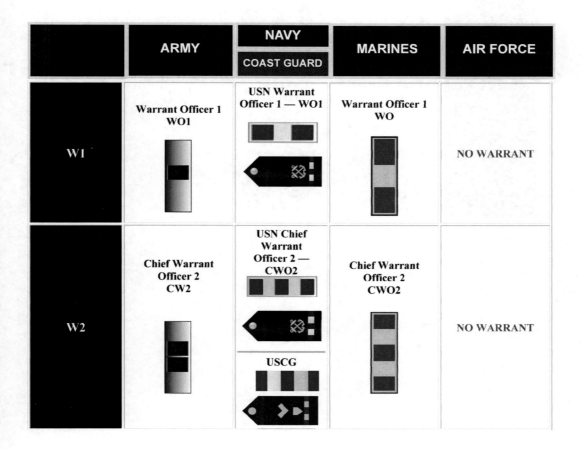

	ARMY	NAVY / COAST GUARD	MARINES	AIR FORCE
W1	Warrant Officer 1 WO1	USN Warrant Officer 1 — WO1	Warrant Officer 1 WO	NO WARRANT
W2	Chief Warrant Officer 2 CW2	USN Chief Warrant Officer 2 — CWO2 / USCG	Chief Warrant Officer 2 CWO2	NO WARRANT

W3	Chief Warrant Officer 3 CW3	USN Chief Warrant Officer 3 — CWO3 **USCG**	Chief Warrant Officer 3 CWO3	NO WARRANT
W4	Chief Warrant Officer 4 CW4	USN Chief Warrant Officer 4 — CWO4 **USCG**	Chief Warrant Officer 4 CWO4	NO WARRANT
W5	Chief Warrant Officer CW5	USN Chief Warrant Officer CWO5	Chief Warrant Officer 5 CWO5	NO WARRANT

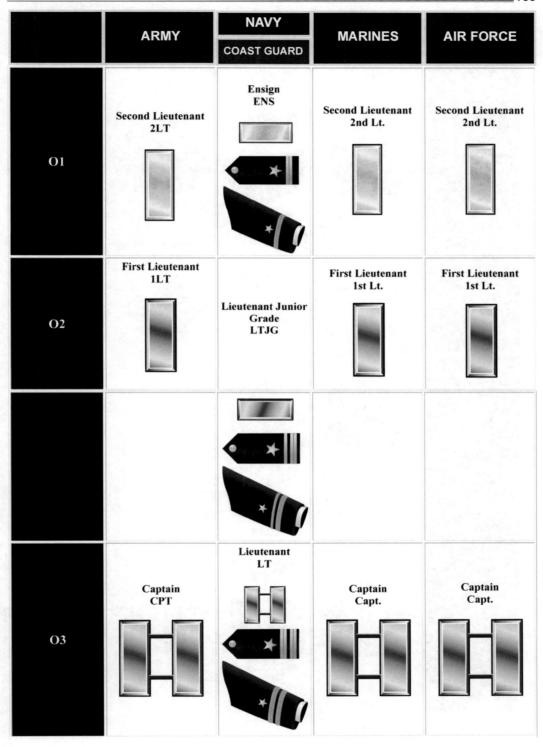

	ARMY	NAVY / COAST GUARD	MARINES	AIR FORCE
O1	Second Lieutenant 2LT	Ensign ENS	Second Lieutenant 2nd Lt.	Second Lieutenant 2nd Lt.
O2	First Lieutenant 1LT	Lieutenant Junior Grade LTJG	First Lieutenant 1st Lt.	First Lieutenant 1st Lt.
O3	Captain CPT	Lieutenant LT	Captain Capt.	Captain Capt.

O4	Major MAJ 	Lieutenant Commander LCDR 	Major Maj. 	Major Maj.
O5	Lieutenant Colonel LTC	Commander CDR	Lieutenant Colonel Lt. Col. 	Lieutenant Colonel Lt. Col.
O6	Colonel COL 	Captain CAPT 	Colonel Col. 	Colonel Col.

O7	**Brigadier General** **BG** 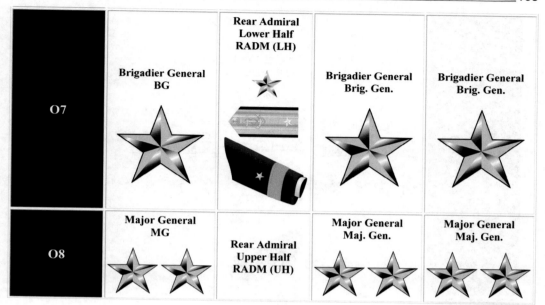	**Rear Admiral** **Lower Half** **RADM (LH)**	**Brigadier General** **Brig. Gen.**	**Brigadier General** **Brig. Gen.**
O8	**Major General** **MG**	**Rear Admiral** **Upper Half** **RADM (UH)**	**Major General** **Maj. Gen.**	**Major General** **Maj. Gen.**

O10	General GEN Army Chief of Staff	Admiral ADM Chief of Naval Operations and Commandant of the Coast Guard	General Gen. Commandant of the Marine Corps	General Gen. Air Force Chief of Staff
	General of the Army (Reserved for wartime only)	Fleet Admiral (Reserved for wartime only)		General of the Air Force (Reserved for wartime only)

Enlisted Insignia

	ARMY	NAVY COAST GUARD	MARINES	AIR FORCE

The **U.S. Coast Guard** is a part of the Department of Transportation in peacetime and the Navy in times of war. Coast Guard rank insignia are the same as the Navy except for color and the seaman recruit rank, which has one stripe.

	ARMY	NAVY / COAST GUARD	MARINES	AIR FORCE
E1	Private	Seaman Recruit (SR)	Private	Airman Basic TOP
E2	Private E-2 (PV2)	Seaman Apprentice (SA)	Private First Class (PFC)	Airman (Amn) TOP
E3	Private First Class (PFC)	Seaman (SN)	Lance Corporal (LCpl)	Airman First Class (A1C) TOP

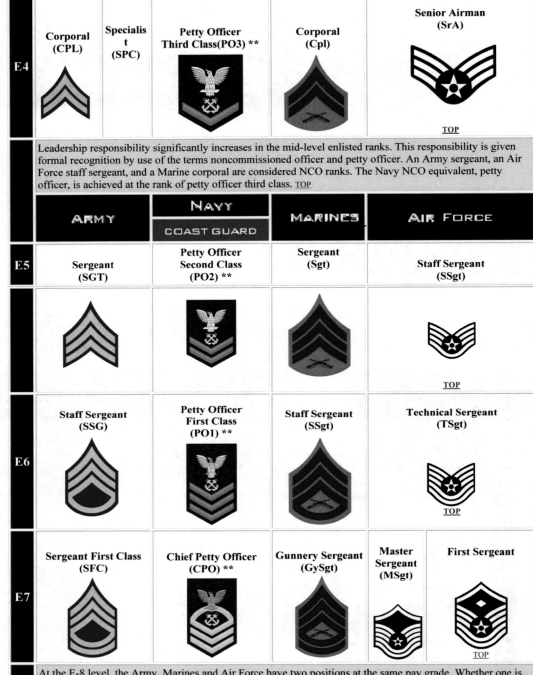

		E4
Corporal (CPL)	Specialist (SPC)	Petty Officer Third Class(PO3) **	Corporal (Cpl)	Senior Airman (SrA)

TOP

Leadership responsibility significantly increases in the mid-level enlisted ranks. This responsibility is given formal recognition by use of the terms noncommissioned officer and petty officer. An Army sergeant, an Air Force staff sergeant, and a Marine corporal are considered NCO ranks. The Navy NCO equivalent, petty officer, is achieved at the rank of petty officer third class. TOP

ARMY	NAVY / COAST GUARD	MARINES	AIR FORCE
E5 Sergeant (SGT)	Petty Officer Second Class (PO2) **	Sergeant (Sgt)	Staff Sergeant (SSgt)

TOP

Staff Sergeant (SSG)	Petty Officer First Class (PO1) **	Staff Sergeant (SSgt)	Technical Sergeant (TSgt)
E6			

TOP

Sergeant First Class (SFC)	Chief Petty Officer (CPO) **	Gunnery Sergeant (GySgt)	Master Sergeant (MSgt)	First Sergeant
E7				

TOP

At the E-8 level, the Army, Marines and Air Force have two positions at the same pay grade. Whether one is, for example, a senior master sergeant or a first sergeant in the Air Force depends on the person's job. The same is true for the positions at the E-9 level. Marine Corps master gunnery sergeants and sergeants major receive the same pay but have different responsibilities. All told, E-8s and E-9s have 15 to 30 years on the job, and are commanders' senior advisers for enlisted matters.

A third E-9 element is the senior enlisted person of each service. The sergeant major of the Army, the sergeant major of the Marine Corps, the master chief petty officer of the Navy and the chief master sergeant of the Air Force are the spokespersons of the enlisted force at the highest levels of their services. TOP

	ARMY		NAVY / COAST GUARD		MARINES			AIR FORCE		
E8	Master Sergeant (MSG)	First Sergeant (1SG)	Senior Chief Petty Officer (SCPO) **		Master Sergeant (MSgt)	First Sergeant	Senior Master Sergeant (SMSgt)	First Sergeant		
								TOP		
E9	Sergeant Major (SGM)	Command Sergeant Major (CSM)	Master Chief Petty Officer (MCPO) ** ***	Fleet/Command Master Chief Petty Officer ** ***	Sergeant Major (SgtMaj)	Master Gunnery Sergeant (MGySgt)	Chief Master Sergeant (CMSgt)	First Sergeant	Command Chief Master Sergeant (CCM)	
									TOP	
E9	Sergeant Major of the Army (SMA)		Master Chief Petty Officer of the Navy (MCPON) and Coast Guard (MCPOCG) ** ***		Sergeant Major of the Marine Corps (SgtMajMC)		Chief Master Sergeant of the Air Force (CMSAF)			

SOURCE: http://www.defenselink.mil/specials/insignias/enlisted.html

Video Resources

All Quiet on the Western Front (1930)	Combatant's moral conflicts during WWI
Best Years of Our Lives, The (1946)	Veteran's readjustment post-WWII
Brothers (2009)	Former OEF POW thought to be dead returns to his family; film chronicles his struggle with PTSD and reintegrating back into family life
Black Hawk Down (2001)	Realistic depiction of urban warfare in 1993 during Operation Enduring Freedom in Somalia
Full Metal Jacket (1987)	Effects of military mindset on Vietnam era Marines
Gunner Palace (2004)	Documentary of the lives soldiers in occupied Baghdad during the current Gulf War
Hamburger Hill (1987)	Realistic portrayal of combat in Vietnam during 1969
Home of the Brave (2006)	Veteran's adjustment after redeployment from current Gulf War
Hurt Locker, The (2008)	Film about a three-man United States Army Explosive Ordnance Disposal (EOD) team during the Iraq war
Jarhead (2005)	Film based on the book that chronicles the experiences of Marines in Saudi Arabia during the first Gulf War.
Pearl Harbor (2001)	Action war film of the Japanese attack on the Pearl Harbor Naval base and the subsequent Doolittle Raid, both during WWII
Platoon (1986)	Realistic portray of life among infantry soldiers during Vietnam 1967-1968

Saving Private Ryan (1998)	Realistic depiction of combat during WWII 1944
Thin Red Line, The (1998)	Fictional story of U.S. forces during the Battle of Guadalcanal during WWII
Turtles Can Fly (2005)	Impact of the current Gulf War on the lives of Kurdish children living on the Iraqi-Turkish border.
We Were Soldiers (2002)	Very realistic depiction of first major combat engagement between US and American soldiers during the Vietnam War.

REFERENCES

American Legion Guide. (2008). Women veterans: Identifying risks, services, prevention. Retrieved from http://www.legion.org/documents/pdf/womensguide.pdf

American Psychiatric Association. (2000). *Diagnostic and statistical manual of mental disorders: Text Revision* (4th ed.). Arlington, VA.: American Psychiatric Association.

American Psychiatric Association. (2004). *Practice guideline for the treatment of patients with acute stress disorder and post traumatic stress disorder.* Arlington, VA.: American Psychiatric Association Practice Guidelines.

Anestis, M., Bryan, C., Cornette, M., & Joiner, T. (2009). Understanding suicidal behavior in the military: An evaluation of Joiner's Interpersonal-Psychological Theory of suicidal behavior in two case studies of active duty post-deployers. *Journal of Mental Health Counseling,* 31(7), 60-75.

Arkowitz, H., & Westra, H. A. (2009). Introduction to the special series on motivational interviewing and psychotherapy. *Journal of Clinical Psychology: In session,* 65(11), 1149-1155. doi: 10.1002/jclp.20640

Army. (2010). *Health promotion, risk reduction, suicide prevention report 2010.* Washington D.C.: United States Army.

Avant, D. D. (2005). *The market for force: The consequences for privatizing security.* New York: Cambridge University Press.

Barnett, F. R., Tovar, D. H., & Shultz, R. H. (1984). *Special operations in U.S. strategy.* New York: National Defense University Press in cooperation with the National Strategy Information Center Inc.

Beck, A. T. (1976). *Cognitive therapy and emotional disorders.* New York: International University Press.

Boot, M. (2002). *Everything you think you know about the American way of war is wrong. E-notes.* Philadelphia, PA: Foreign Policy Research Institute.

Bray, R. M., & Hourani, L. L. (2007). Substance use trends among active duty military personnel: Findings from the United States Department of Defense Health Related Behavior Surveys, 1980-2005. *Addiction*, 10, 1092-1101. doi: 10.1111/j.1360-0443.2007.01841.x

Burke, H. S., Degeneffe, C. E., & Olney, M. F. (2009). A new disability for rehabilitation counselors: Iraq War veterans with Traumatic Brain Injury and Post-Traumatic Stress Disorder. *Journal of Rehabilitation,* 75(3), 5-14.

Byrne, C. A., & Riggs, D. S. (1996). The cycle of trauma: Relationship aggression in male veterans with symptoms of Post-Traumatic Stress Disorder. *Violence and Victims,* 11(3), 213-226.

Carlson, E. B. (1997). *Trauma assessments: A clinician's guide*. New York: Guilford Press.

CBS News. (2007). Suicide epidemic among veterans: A CBS News investigation uncovers a suicide rate for veterans twice that of other Americans. CBS News. Retrieved from http://www.cbsnews.com/stories/2007/11/13/cbsnews_investigates/main3496471.shtml?tag=mncol;lst;1

CBS News. (2010). U.S. troops injury in Afghanistan already near last years total. *CBS News*. Retrieved from http://www.cbsnews.com/8301-503543_162-20010672-503543.html

Cebrowski, A. K. (2001). President's Forum. Naval War College Review, Summer 2001, Vol. LIV, 3, pp. 7-10.

Center for Military Readiness. (2002). The homosexual exclusion law vs. the Clinton "don't ask, don't tell" policy. Retrieved from http://cmrlink.org

Center for Women Veterans. (2010). Women veterans population. Washington D.C.: Department of Veterans Affairs. Retrieved from http://www1.va.gov/womenvet/statistics.asp

Central Intelligence Agency. (2004). The world fact book 2004. Office of Public Affairs. Washington, D.C.: CIA.

Cherniss, C. (1993). The role of professional self-efficacy in the etiology and amelioration of burnout. In W. B. Schsufeli, C. Maslach, & T. Marek (Eds.), *Professional burnout: Recent developments in theory and research* (pp. 53-69). Washington D.C.: Taylor & Francis.

CNN Timeline. (2004). Focus on Kosovo: A timeline of tensions. CNN In-Depth Specials. Retrieved from http://www.cnn.com/SPECIALS/1998/10/kosovo/timeline/

Cohen, E. A. (2001, November 20). What's in a name: World War IV. Let's call this conflict what it is. *Wall Street Journal*. Retrieved from http://www.opinionJournal.com/editorial/feature.html?d+95001493

Coll, J. E., Weiss, E. L, & Draves, P. R. (2010, October). *The impact of military cultural awareness, experience, attitudes, and education on clinician self-efficacy in the treatment of veterans*. Paper presented at the Fifty-Sixth Annual Council of Social Work Education Conference, Portland, OR.

Coll, J. E., Weiss, E. L., & Yarvis, J. (in press). No one leaves unchanged: Insights for civilian mental health care professionals into the military experience and culture. *Journal of Social Work in Healthcare.*

Collaborative Research on Organizations. (2009). Company profile: Halliburton. Retrieved from http://www.crocodyl.org/wiki/halliburton

Congressional Budget Office. (2006). A CBO Study: *Recruiting, retention, and future levels of military personnel* (Report No. 2777). Retrieved from http://www.cbo.gov/ftpdocs/76xx/doc7626/10-05 -Recruiting.pdf

Cook, M. L. (2004). *The moral warrior: Ethics and service in the U.S. military.* New York: State University of New York Press.

Coxell, A., & King, M. (2002). Gender, sexual orientation, and sexual assault. In J. Petrak & B. Hedge (Eds.), *The trauma of sexual assault, prevention, and practice* (pp. 45-68). Chichester, England, John Wiley & Sons, Ltd.

Davenport, M. (1987). Professionals or hired guns? Loyalties are the difference. In M. M.Watkin, K.Wenker and J. Kempf (Eds.) *Military ethics: Reflections on principles—the profession of arms, military   leadership, ethical practices, war and morality, educating the citizen soldier* (pp. 5-12). Washington,

D.C.: National Defense University Press.

Davey, M. (2004). Former G.I.'s ordered to war, fight not to go. *The New York Times.* Retrieved from http://www.nytimes.com/2004/11/16/national/16reserves.html

Davidson, J. R., Bernik, M., Conner, K. M., Friedman, M. J., Jobson, K. O., Kim, Y., . . . Zohar, J. (2005). A new treatment algorithm for Posttraumatic Stress Disorder. *Psychiatric Annals, 35*(11), 887-898.

Davidson, J. R., Weisler, R. H., Butterfield, M. E., Casat, C. D., Conner, M., Barnett, S., and van Meter, S. (2003). Mirtazapine vs. placebo in Posttraumatic Stress Disorder: A pilot trial. *Biol. Psychiatry, 53*, 188-191.

Davis, M., Barad, M., Otto, M., & Southwick, S., (2007). Combining pharmacotherapy with cognitive behavioral therapy: Traditional and new approaches. *Journal of Traumatic Stress, 19*(5), 571-581. doi: 10.1002/jts.20149

Defense Jobs. (2004). Officer Entry, Graduate Only, Chaplain. (Army). Retrieved from http::// www.defensejobs.gov.au/careers_explorer/Army151.html

Defense and Veterans Brain Injury Center. (2010). TBI Numbers. Retrieved from http://www. dvbic.org/TBI-Numbers.aspx

DeGorge, P. T. (1987). A code of ethics for officers. In M. M.Watkin, K. Wenker, and J. Kempf (Eds.). Military ethics: Reflections on principles—the profession of arms, *military leadership, ethical practices, war and morality, educating the citizen soldier* (pp. 13-29).Washington, D.C.: National Defense University.

Department of the Army. (2007). *Reassignment* (Army regulation 600-8-11). Washington, D.C.: Headquarters, Department of the Army.

Department of Defense. (2001). *Military careers: A guide to military occupations.* Washington, D.C.: U.S. Department of Defense.

Department of Defense. (2006). Operation Iraqi Freedom (OIF) U.S. casualty status: Fatalities as of August 9, 2006. Retrieved from http://osd.dtic.mil/news/casualty. pdf

Department of Defense. (2010a). Contracts. Retrieved from http://www.defense.gov/ Contracts/

Department of Defense. (2010b). Operation Iraqi Freedom U.S. casualty status/ Operation Enduring Freedom U.S. casualty status. Washington D.C.: Department of Defense. Retrieved from http://www.defense.gov/news/casualty.pdf

Department of Defense. (2010c). Reserve components: Noble Eagle/ Enduring Freedom/ Iraqi Freedom. Washington D.C.: Department of Defense.

Department of Defense. (2010d). "Road map for success" step one: Determine your best benefit. Retrieved from https://www.gibill.va.gov/apply-for-benefits/road-map/1-determine-your-best-benefit.html

Department of Defense Sexual Assaults Prevention and Response Office. (2010). *Fiscal year 2009 report on sexual assault in the military.* Washington D.C.: Department of Defense.

Department of Veterans Affairs. (2003, November). *V A Programs for Homeless Veterans. Fact Sheet.* Office of Public Relations, Media Relations. Washington, D.C.: Department of Veterans Affairs.

Department of Veterans Affairs. (2004, May). *Facts about the Department of Veterans Affairs. Fact Sheet.* Office of Public Relations, Media Relations. Washington D.C.: Department of Veterans Affairs.

Department of Defense and Veterans Affairs. (2007). Treatment of PTSD. Retrieved from http://www.ptsd.va.gov/public/pages/treatment-ptsd.asp

Department of Veterans Affairs. (2009a, January). *Facts about the Department of Veterans Affairs Fact Sheet.* Office of Public Affairs, Media Relations. Washington D.C.: Department of Veterans Affairs.

Department of Veterans Affairs. (2009b, May). Fast facts: President's 2010 budget for VA. Washington D.C.: Department of Veterans Affairs.

Department of Veterans Affairs. (2010a). *Department of Veterans Affairs National Cemeteries.* Washington D.C.: Department of Veterans Affairs. Retrieved from http://www. va.gov/

Department of Veterans Affairs. (2010b). *Did you know? Center for women veterans.* Washington D.C.: Department of Veterans Affairs.

Department of Veterans Affairs. (2010c). *Funding highlights: The budget for fiscal year 2011.* Washington .C.: Department of Veterans Affairs.

Department of Veterans Affairs. (2010d). GI Bill history: Born of controversy: The GI Bill of Rights. Washington D.C.: Department of Veterans Affairs.

Department of Veterans Affairs. (2010e). *VA 2011 budget fast facts.* Washington D.C.: Department of Veterans Affairs.

Department of Veterans Affairs. (2010f). *What is the Post 9/11 GI Bill?* Washington D.C.: Department of Veterans Affairs.

Department of Veterans Affairs. (2010g). *Yellow Ribbon Program.* Washington D.C.: Department of Veterans Affairs.

Department of Veterans Affairs & Department of Defense. (2004). *VA/DoD clinical practice guideline for the management of post-traumatic stress.* Washington DC: Department of Defense.

Department of Veterans Affairs, and National Center for PTSD. (2002). *Posttraumatic Stress Disorder: Implications for primary care.* Washington D.C.: Department of Veterans Affairs.

Disabled American Veterans. (2008). Issue brief: Veterans and substance abuse. Retrieved from http://www.standup4vets.org/PressRoom/IssueBriefs.html

Duke, L. (1997, August 16) U.S. Military role in Rwanda greater than disclosed. *The Washington Post, A01,* Retrieved from http://www.udayton.edu/Rwanda/articles/usrole.html

Echevarria, A. J., II. (2004). *Toward an American way of war. Strategic Studies Institute Monograph.* Carlisle, PA: U.S. Army War College.

Elshtain, J. B. (1987). *Women and war.* New York: Basic Books, Inc.

Environmental Agents Service. (2002a, March). *Afghanistan veterans: Information for veterans who served in Afghanistan.* Washington D.C.: Veterans Health Administration, Department of Veterans Affairs, 1-4.

Environmental Agents Service. (2002b, March). *Military service in the Afghanistan War: Questions and answers about health concerns of veterans and their families.* Washington D.C.: Veterans Health Administration, Department of Veterans Affairs, 1-4.

Evers, K. (2007). Perspectives on memory manipulation: Using Beta-blockers to cure Posttraumatic Stress Disorder. *Cambridge Quarterly of Healthcare Ethics, 16,* 138-146. doi: 10.1017/S0963180107070168

Faiver, C., Eisengart, S., and Colona, R. (2000). *The counselor intern's handbook.* (2nd ed.). Belmont, CA: Brooks/Cole.

Farrell, E. (2005). GI Blues. Retrieved from http://chronicle.com/weekly/v51/i36/36a03101.htm.

Ficarrotta, J. C. (1993). Careerism in the military services: A moral analysis of its nature, types, and contributing causes. In J. C. Gaston and J.B. Hietala (Eds.), *Ethics and national defense: The timeless issues* (pp. 35-55). Washington, D.C.: National Defense University.

Figley, C. R. (1985). From victim to survivor: Social responsibility in the wake of catastrophe. In C.R. Figley (Ed.), *Trauma and its wake: The study and treatment of Posttraumatic Stress Disorder* (pp. 398-416). New York: Brunner/Mazel.

Ferroggiaro, W. (2004). The U.S. and the genocide in Rwanda 1994. Information, intelligence and the U.S. response. The National Security Archive. Retrieved from http://www.gwu.edu/nsarchiv/NSAEBB/NSAEBB117/

Foa, E. B., Hembree, E. A., & Rothbaum, B. O. (2007). *Prolonged exposure therapy for PTSD: Emotional processing of traumatic experiences therapist guide.* New York: Oxford University Press.

Foa, E. B., Keane, T. M., & Friedman, M. J. (Eds.) (2000). *Effective treatment for PTSD: Practice guidelines from the International Society for Traumatic Stress Studies.* New York: Guildford.

Foster, R. (2010). Stand Down's information page about homelessness. Retrieved from http://www.standown.org/homeless.html

Fox News. (2010, August 31). Transcript: President Barrack Obama's oval office speech on Iraq. Retrieved from http://www.foxnews.com/politics/2010/08/31/transcript-president-obamas-oval-office-speech-iraq/

Friedman, M. J. (2003). PTSD diagnosis and treatment for mental health clinicians. In M. J. Scott and S. 'Palmer (Eds.) *Trauma and post-traumatic stress disorder* (pp. 1-14). Thousand Oaks, California: Sage Publications.

Friedman, M. J, Schnurr, P. P., and McDonagh-Coyle, A. (1994). Post-traumatic Stress Disorder in the military veteran. *Psychiatric Clinics of North America*, 17(2), 265-277.

Gabriel, R. (1987). Legitimate avenues of military protest. In M. M.Watkin, K.Wenker, and J. Kempf (Eds.), *Military ethics: Reflections on principles—the profession of arms, military leadership, ethical practices, war and morality, educating the citizen soldier* (pp. 171-175). Washington, D.C.: National Defense University Press.

Gaston, J. C. and Hietala, J. B. (1993). *Ethics and national defense: The timeless issues.* Washington, D.C.: National Defense University

Gerlock, A. (1996). An anger management model for veterans with PTSD. *National Center for Post-Traumatic Stress Disorder Clinical Quarterly,* 6(3), 61-64.

Gibbs, R. D. (2004). *Determining an appropriate force sizing paradigm for the U.S. Army* (Masters Thesis). Carlisle: U.S. Army War College, 2.

Global Security. (2004). World War IV [World War 4]. Retrieved from http://www.gloabalsecurity.org/military/ops/world_war_4htm

Grossman, D. (1996). *On killing: The psychological consequences of learning to kill in war and society.* New York: Little, Brown and Company.

Harben, J. (2006). Mental health advisory team III findings released. U.S. Army Medical Department: Army Medicine. Washington D.C.: Department of Defense. Retrieved from http://www.armymedicine.army.mil/news/releases/20061219_mhatiii.cfm

Hayes, S. C., & Smith, S. (2005). *Get out of your mind and into your life: The new acceptance and commitment therapy.* Oakland, CA: New Harbinger.

Hellinger, D., & Judd, D. R. (1991). *The democratic façade.* Pacific Grove, CA: Brooks-Cole

Herman, J. L. (1992). *Trauma and Recovery: The aftermath of violence.* New York: Basic Books.

Herschell, A. D., Kogan, J. N., Celedonia, K. L., Gavin, J. G., & Stein, B. D. (2009). Understanding community mental health administrators' perspectives on Dialectical Behavioral Therapy implementation. *Psychiatric Services, 60*(7), 989-992.

Hodge, S., & Canter, D. (1998). Victims and perpetrators of male sexual assault. *Journal of Interpersonal Violence, 13*(2), 222-239.

Holm, T. (1992). Statistics and data: The national survey of Indian Vietnam Veterans. In *Report of The Working Group on American Indian Vietnam Era Veterans* (pp. 25-36). Washington D.C.: Readjustment Counseling Service, Department of Veterans Affairs.

Hooker, R. D. (2003). Soldiers of the state: Reconsidering American civil-military relations. *Parameters, U.S. Army War College Quarterly, 33*(4), 4-18.

Huffington, A. (2010, June 6). Halliburton, KBR, and Iraq war contracting: A history so far. St. Petersburg Times: *PolitiFact.* Retrieved from http://www.politifact.com/truth-o-meter/statements/2010/jun/09/arianna-huffington/halliburton-kbr-and-iraq-war-contracting-history-s/

Hyer, L, McCranie, E. W., & Peralme, L. (1993). Psychotherapeutic treatment of chronic PTSD. *The National Center for Posttraumatic Stress Disorder PTSD Research Quarterly,* 4(2), 1-3.

Iraq Coalition Casualty Count. (2010). Iraq Coalition Casualties: U.S. wounded totals. Retrieved from http://icasualties.org/Iraq/USCasualtiesByState.aspx

Jeffer, E. K. (1979, August). Psychiatric Evaluations for Administrative Purposes. *Military Medicine 144, 506-528. as cited in Laforet, E.G. (1993) Limits of Loyalty and Obedience: Does the Military Physician Serve two Masters* (pp.101-111) In J. C. Gaston and J.B. Hietala (Eds.), *Ethics and national defense: The timeless issues* (pp.101-111). Washington, D.C.: National Defense University.

Joint Chiefs of Staff. (1997). *Joint Strategy Review* (p. 2.).Washington, D.C.: Joint Staff

Johnson, E. (1987). Why don't we follow rules. In M. M.Watkin, K.Wenker, and J. Kempf (Eds.), *Military ethics: Reflections on principles—the profession of arms, military leadership, ethical practices, war and morality, educating the citizen soldier* (pp. 125-138). Washington, D.C.: National Defense University Press.

Keane, T. M., Fairbank, J. A., Caddell, J. M., Zimering, R. T., Taylor, K. L., & Mora, C. A. (1989). Brief reports: Clinical evaluation of a measure to assess combat exposure. *Journal of Consulting and Clinical Psychology, 1*(1), 53-55.

Kegan, J., & Holmes, R. (1985). Soldiers: *A history of men in battle.* New York: Elizabeth Shifton Books, Viking Penguin Inc.

Kennedy, A. (2004, June). Emotional cycle of deployment: Information for civilian counselors about the military family. *Counseling Today, 46*(12), 1-45.

Knake, B. (1995, March/April). What to say/not say to the grieving. *The Forum,* 13-14.

Knull, D. P. (1971, July). The Physician-patient privilege, Article 31, and the *Military Doctor. Military Medicine,* 136, 640-643. as cited in Laforet, E.G. (1993) *Limits of Loyalty and Obedience: Does the Military Physician Serve two Masters* (pp.101-111), In J. C. Gaston and J. B. Hietala (Eds.) *Ethics and national defense: The timeless issues* (pp.101-111), Washington, D.C.: National Defense University.

Kornblut, A. (2010, August 31). Obama declares the war in Iraq is over. *The Washington Post.* Retrieved from http://www.washingtonpost.com/wpdyn/content/article/2010/08/31/AR2010083104496.html?sid=ST2010083106297

Kubler-Ross, E. (1969). *On death and dying.* New York: Macmillan.

Kulka, R. A., Schlenger, W. E., Fairbank, J. A., Housy, R. L., Jordan, B. K., Marmar, C. R. and Weiss, D.S. (1990a). *The National Vietnam Veterans Readjustment Study. Table of findings and Technical appendices.* New York: Brunner/Mazel.

Kulka, R. A., Schlenger, W. E., Fairbank, J. A., Housy, R. L., Jordan, B. K., Marmar, C. R. and Weiss, D.S. (1990b). *Trauma and the Vietnam War Generation: Report of findings from the National Vietnam Veterans Readjustment Study.* New York: Brunner/Mazel.

Leinwand, D. (2009). Courts work with VA, bar to help vets with legal problems. *USA Today,* 03A.

Linehan, M. M., & Heard, H. L. (1992). Dialectical behavior therapy for borderline personality disorder. In J. F. Clarkin, E. Marziali, & H. Munroe-Blum (Eds.), *Borderline personality disorder: Clinical and empirical perspectives* (pp. 248-267). New York: Guilford Press.

Litz, B. and Orsillo, S. M. (2003). The returning veteran of the Iraq War: Background issues and assessment guidelines. *In The Iraq War Clinician Guide* (pp.1-13), Department of Veterans Affairs, Palo Alto, CA: The National Center for Post-Traumatic Stress Disorder.

Loo, C. M. (1994). Race-related trauma and PTSD: The Asian American Vietnam veteran. *Journal of Traumatic Stress, 7,* 637-649.

Mahnken, T. G. (2001). Transforming the U.S. armed forces: Rhetoric or reality? *The Naval War College Review, LIV 3,* 85-99.

Marmar, C. R., Weiss, D. S, and Pynoos, R. B. (1995). Dynamic psychotherapy of post traumatic stress disorder. In M. J. Friedman, D. S. Charney, & A. Y. Deutch (Eds.), *Neurobiological and clinical consequences of stress: From normal adaptation to PTSD.* New York: Raven Press.

Marine Battle Skills Training (MBST) Handbook. (1995). Book 4 SSGT-GYSGT. Individual Combat Basic Tasks. Albany, Georgia: Marine Corps Publication Distribution System. Marine Corps Institute.

Maslach, C., & Jackson, S. E. (1986). T*he Maslach burnout inventory.* Palo Alto, CA.: Consulting Psychologists Press.

Mason, P. T., & Kreger, R. (2008). Stop walking on eggshells: *Taking your life back when someone you know has Borderline Personality Disorder.* Oakland, CA.: New Harbinger Publications, Inc.

Mateczun, J., and Holmes, E. (1996). Return, readjustment, and reintegration: The three R's of family reunion. In R.Ursano and A. Norwood (Eds.), *Emotional aftermath of the Persian Gulf War: Veterans, families, communities, and nations* (pp. 369-392). Washington, DC: American Psychiatric Press, Inc.

Matsuoka, J., Hamada, R., Kilauna, W., & Coalson, R. (1992). Asian-Pacific American Vietnam veterans: An exploratory study of wartime experiences and post-war adjustment. *Journal of Multicultural Social Work, 2*, 103-111.

McCann, I. L., & Perlman, L. A. (1990). Vicarious traumatization: A framework for understanding thepsychological effects of working with victims. *Journal of Traumatic Stress, 3*(1), 131-149.

Medical News Today. (2008, March 29). VA reaches out to women veterans. Retrieved from http://www.medicalnewstoday.com/articles/101970.php

Megis, M. C. (2003). Unorthodox thoughts about asymmetric warfare. *Parameters. U.S. Army War College Quarterly, XXXIII2(99)*, 4-18.

Merzoff, W. J. (2010). Social workers link veterans to a range of services. Retrieved From http://www.military.com/Careers/Content1?file=careersArticlesVeteransServic es.htm&area=Reference

Meyer, S. E. (2003). Carcass of dead policies: The irrelevance of NATO. Parameters: *U.S. War College Quarterly*, 33(4), 83-97.

Military. (2010a). Chaplains. Retrieved from http://www.military.com/benefits/resources/ family-support/chaplains

Military. (2010b). VA health care eligibility. Retrieved from http://www.military.com/benefits/ veterans-health-care/va-health-care-eligibility

Miller, L. J. (2008). Prazosin for the treatment of posttraumatic stress disorder sleep disturbances. Pharmacotherapy, 28(5), 656-666.

Miller, S. (200a7, January-February). Healing body and brain. *Minnesota,* 106(3), 24-29.

Miller, T. C. (2007b). Private contractors outnumber U.S. troops in Iraq. *Los Angeles Times*. Retrieved from http://articles.latimes.com

Miller, W. R., & Rollnick, S. (2002). *Motivational Interviewing: Preparing people for change* (2nd ed.). New York: The Guilford Press.

Miskel, J. F. (2001). Being there matters- But where? *Naval War College Review, LIV*(3), 25-39.

Monson, C. M., Schnurr, P. P., Resick, P. A., Friedman, M. J., Young-Xu, Y., & Stevens, S. P. (2006). Cognitive processing therapy for veterans with military-related posttraumatic stress disorder. *Journal of Consulting and Clinical Psychology, 74*(5), 898-907.

Moxon, A. (1985). U.S. Reserve Forces: The Achilles Heel of the all Volunteer Force? In B.J. William III (Ed.), *The Guard and Reserve in the Total Force* (pp. 91-113). Washington, D.C.: National Defense University Press.

Munroe, J. F., Shay, J., Fisher, L., Makary, C., Rapperport, K., & Zimering, R. (1995). Preventing compassion fatigue: A team treatment model. In C. Figley (Ed.), Compassion fatigue: *Coping with secondary traumatic stress disorder in those who treat the traumatized* (pp. 209-231). New York: Brunner-Routledge.

Murphy, R. T. (2008). Enhancing combat veterans motivation to change posttraumatic stress disorder and other problem behaviors. In H. Arkowitz, H. A. Westra, W. R. Miller, & S. Rollnick (Eds.), *Motivational interviewing the treatment of psychological problems* (pp. 57-84). New York: The Guilford Press.

National Center for PTSD. (2005). Returning from the war zone: A guide for military personnel. Retrieved from http://ncptsd.va.gov/ncmain/ncdocs/manuals/GuideforMilitary.pdf

National Center for PTSD. (2010). Intimate partner violence. Retrieved from http://www.ptsd.va.gov/public/pages/domestic-violence.asp

National Center for Veterans Analysis and Statistics, DVA Information Technology Center, Health Services Training Report. (2010). VA benefits and health care utilization. Retrieved from www1.va.gov/VETDATA/Pocket-Card/4X6_spring10_sharepoint.pdf

National Coalition for Homeless Veterans. (2010). Department of Veterans Affairs releases 2009 CHALENG Report. Retrieved from http://www.nchv.org/news_article.cfm?id=771

National Conference on Ministry to the Armed Forces. (2010). How to become a chaplain. Retrieved from http://www.ncmaf.org/chaplain.htm

National Survey on Drug Use and Health. (2008, November 6). Office of Applied Studies, Substance Abuse and Mental Health Administration (SAMHSA). Retrieved from http://www.oas.samhsa.gov/2k8/veteransDepressed/veteransDepressed.pdf

National Institute of Drug Abuse. (2009). Substance abuse among the military, veterans, and their families. Retrieved from http://www.nida.nih.gov/tib/vet.html

National Veterans Foundation. (2008). Facts about veterans: Needs and solutions. Retrieved from http://www.nvf.org/?q=facts-about-veterans

Neimeyer, R. A. (2000). Narrative disruptions in the construction of the self. In R. A. Neimeyer & J. D. Raskin (Eds.), *Constructions of disorder: Meaning making frameworks for psychotherapy* (pp. 207-242). Washington DC: American Psychological Association.

Neuman, A., & Gamble, S. (1995). Issues in the professional development of psychotherapists: Countertransference and vicarious traumatization in the new trauma therapist. *Psychotherapy, 32*(2), 341-347.

Novaco, R. (1996). Anger treatment and its special challenges. National Center for Posttraumatic Stress Disorder. *Clinical Quarterly, 6*(3), 56-60.

O'Brien, W. V. (1984) Special ops in the 1980s: American moral, legal, political and cultural constraints. In F. R. Bennett, B. H. Tovar, & R. H. Shultz (Eds.), *Special operations in U.S. strategy* (pp. 54-84). New York: National Defense University Press.

Orr, G. E. (1983). *Combat operations C3I: Fundamentals and interactions.* Alabama, Maxwell Air Force Base: Air University Press.

Parson, E. R. (1984). The gook-identification and post-traumatic stress disorder. *Black Psychiatrist of American Quarterly, 25*, 65-85.

Pavlicin, K. M. (2007). *Life after deployment: Military families share reunion stories and advice.* St. Paul, MN: Elva Resa Publishing.

Pearlman, L. A., & Saakvitne, K. W. (1995). Trauma and the therapist: Countertransference and vicarious traumatization in psychotherapy with incest survivors. In C.R. Figley (Ed.), *Coping with secondary traumatic stress disorder in those who treat the traumatized* (pp. 150- 177). New York: W.W. Norton.

Perlman, S. (1995). One analysists journey into darkness: Countertransference resistance to recognizing sexual abuse, ritual abuse, and multiple personality disorders. *Journal of the American Academy of Psychoanalysis, 23*(1), 137-151.

Philbin, E .J and Gould, J. L. (1985). The Guard and Reserve: In Pursuit of Full Integration. In B.J. William III (Ed.), *The Guard and Reserve in the Total Force* (pp.43-57). Washington, D.C.: National Defense University Press.

Pilkington, E. (2010, June). US Military: Women are very much in combat. *The Guardian.* Retrieved from http://www.guardian.co.uk/world/2010/jun/23/us-military-women-in-combat Policy concerning homosexuality in the armed forces. Public Law 103-160- Section 546-107. (2010).

Post-Deployment Health Reassessment (PDHRA) Program Task Force Report. (2007). Montana Veterans Affairs Division, Department of Veterans Affairs. Retrieved from http://www.dma.mt.gov/mvad/document/PDHRA.pdf

Price, J. L. (2007). *Findings from the National Vietnam Veterans' Readjustment Study.* Washington D.C.: Department of Veterans Affairs. Retrieved from http://www.va.gov/

Prins, A., Kimerling, R., Cameron, R., Oumiette, P. C., Shaw, J., Thraikill, A., . . . Gusman, F. (1999). The primary care PTSD screen (PC-PTSD). Paper presented at the Fifteenth Annual Meeting of the International Society for Traumatic Stress Studies, Miami, FL.

Prins, A., Kimerling, R, & Leskin, G. (2003). *PTSD in Iraq war veterans: Implications for primary care. The Iraq War Clinician Guide* (pp.33-36). Department of Veterans Affairs, Palo Alto, CA: The National Center for Post-Traumatic Stress Disorder.

Ramchand, R., Karney, B. R., Osilla, K. C., Burns, R. M., & Caldarone, L. B. (2008). Prevalence of PTSD, depression, and TBI among returning servicemembers. In T. Tanielian, & L. H. Jaycox (Eds.), *Invisible woulds of war: Psychologyical and cognitive injuries, their consequences, and services to assist recovery.* Santa Monica, CA.: RAND Corporation.

Ramchand, R., Schell, T. L., Karney, B. R., Osilla, K. C., Burns, R. M., & Calderone, L. B. (2010). Disparate prevalence estimates of PTSD among service members who served in Iraq and Afghanistan: Possible explanations. *Journal of Traumatic Stress, 23*(1), 59-68. doi: 10.1002/jts

Raskind, M. A. (2009). Pharmacologic Treatment of PTSD. In P. J. Shiromani et al (Eds.), *Post Traumatic Stress Disorder: Basic science and clinical practice* (pp. 337-361). doi: 10.1007/978-1-60327-329-9_16

Raskind, M. A., Peskind, E. R., Hoff, D. J., Hart, K. L., Holmes, H. A., Warren, D., . . .McFall, M. E. (2007). A parallel group placebo controlled study of Prazosin for trauma nightmares and sleep disturbance in combat veterans with Post-Traumatic Stress Disorder. *Biological Psychiatry*, 61, 928-934. doi: 10.1016/j.biopsych.2006.06.032

Raymond, D. A. (1993). Soldiers, unjust wars, and treason. In J. C. Gaston and J.B. Hietala (Eds.), *Ethics and national defense: The timeless issues* (pp.57-74). Washington, D.C.: National Defense University.

Reeve, S. (2001, December 16). U.S returning to a nightmare called Somalia. *The San Francisco Chronicle.* Retrieved from http://www.sfgate.com/cgi-bin/article. cgi?file=/c/a/2001/12/16/MN115488.DTL

Record, J. (2002). *Failed states and casualty phobia: Implication for force structure and technology choices* (Occasional paper no. 18). Center for Strategy and Technology. Air War College, Air University, Maxwell Air Force Base, Alabama.

Rentz, E. D., Gibbs, D. A., Clinton-Sherrod, M., Hardison, J., & Marshall, S. W. (2006). Family violence in the military: A review of the literature. *Trauma, Violence, and Abuse, 7*, 93-108. doi: 10.1177/1524838005285916

Roots, C. (2002, November 20). The role of the military chaplain. Roots on Deck. Retrieved from ttp://www.freemethodistchurch.org/Section/Communications/News%20 Stories/Roots%2... Retrieved 5/17/04

Rothbaum, B. O., Difede, J. & Rizzo, A. (2008). *Therapist treatment manual for virtual reality exposure therapy: Posttraumatic stress Disorder in Iraq Combat Veterans.* Georgia: Virtually Better, Inc.

Ruzek, J., Curran, E., Friedman, M. J, Gusman, F. D., Southwick, S. M., Swales, P., Walser, R. D., Watson, P. J., & Whealin, J. (2003). *Treatment of the returning Iraq war veteran. The Iraq War Clinician Guide* (pp.14-26). Department of Veterans Affairs, Palo Alto, CA: The National Center for Post-Traumatic Stress Disorder.

Sadler, A. (2009). *VA's changing mission: Research focusing of families and caregivers of veterans with trauma.* Washington D.C.: Iowa City VA Medical Center, Department of Veterans Affairs, Office of Research and Development.

Savitsky, L., Illingworth, M., & DuLaney, M. (2009). Civilian social work: Serving the military and veteran populations. *Research Library Core,* 54(4), 327-339.

Sayers, S. L., Farrow, V. A., Ross, J., & Oslin, D. W. (2009). Family problems among recently returned military veterans referred for a mental health evaluation. *Journal of Clinical Psychiatry,* 70, 163-170.

Scahill, J. (2005). CSC/DynCorp. Corp watch: Holding corporations accountable. Retrieved from http://www.corpwatch.org

Scioli, E. R., Otis, J. D., & Keane, T. M. (2010). Psychological problems associated with Operation Enduring Freedom/Operation Iraqi Freedom Deployment. *American Journal of Lifestyle Medicine,* 4(4), 349-359. doi: 10.1177/1559827610362962

Schlenger, W. E., Kulka, R. A., Fairbank, J. A., Hough, R. L., Jordan, B. K., Marmar, C.R. and Weiss, D.S. (1992). The Prevalence of Post-Traumatic Stress Disorder in the Vietnam generation: A multi-method multi-source assessment of psychiatric disorder. *Journal of Traumatic Stress,* 5, pp.333-363.

Scott, W. J. (1993). *The politics of readjustment: Vietnam veterans since the war.* New York: Aldine Transaction.

Servicemembers Legal Defense Network. (2010). About "don't ask, don't tell." Retrieved from http://www.sldn.org/pages/about-dadt

Shapiro, F. (2001). *Eye movement desensitization and reprocessing: Basic principles, protocols and procedures* (2nd ed.). New York: Guilford Press.

Shay, J. (1995). About medications for combat PTSD. Interoffice Memorandum. Boston VA Outpatient Clinic. Boston, Massachusetts.

Sheppard, B. (2001). *A war of nerves: Soldiers and psychiatrists in the twentieth century.* Cambridge, MA.: Harvard University Press.

Sherman, M. D. (2003). The SAFE program: A family psychoeducational curriculum developed in a Veteran's Affairs medical center. *Professional Psychology: Research and Practice,* 34(1), 42-48. doi: 10.1037/0735-7028.34.1.42

Sherman, M. D., Zanotti, D. K., & Jones, D. E. (2005). Key elements in couples therapy with veterans with combat related *posttraumatic stress disorder. Professional Psychology: Research and Practice,* 36(6), 626-633. doi: 10.1037/0735-7028.36.6.626

Simon, J. (1988). *NATO and Warsaw Pact Institutional Development. In J. Simon (Ed.), NATO-WARSAW Pact Force Mobilization* (pp. 31-56). Washington, D.C.: The National Defense University Press.

Singer, P. W. (2004). War, profits, and the vacuum of law: Privatized military firms and international law. *Columbia Journal of Transnational Law, 42*(2), 522-550.

Smith, J. (1985). Individual psychotherapy with Viet Nam veterans. In S. M. Sonnenberg, A. S. Blank, & J. A. Talbot (Eds.), *The trauma of war: Stress and recovery in Viet Nam veterans* (pp.127-163). Washington, DC: American Psychiatric Press, Inc.

Solomon, Z. (1993). *Combat Stress Reactions: The enduring toll of war.* New York: Plenum Press.

Street, A., and Stafford, J. (2003). *Military sexual trauma: Issues in caring for veterans. The Iraq War Clinician Guide* (pp.37-40). Department of Veterans Affairs, Palo Alto, CA.: The National Center for Post-Traumatic Stress Disorder.

Stremlow, M. V. (1986). *A history of the women Marines, 1946-1977.*, Washington, D.C.: History and Museums Division Headquarters, U.S. Marine Corps.

Stenger, C. (2002). *American prisoners of war in WWI, WWII, Korea, Vietnam, Persian Gulf, Somalia, Bosnia, Kosovo and Afghanistan. Statistical data concerning numbers captured, repatriated, and still alive as of January 1, 2002.* Department of Veteran Affairs Advisory Committee of Former Prisoners of War Mental Health Strategic Health Care Group, VHA, DVA, American Ex-Prisoners of War Association: Bethesda, Maryland.

Steury, D. P. (Ed.). (1999). *On the front lines of the cold war: Documents on the Intelligence war in Berlin, 1946 to 1961.* CIA History Staff. Washington, DC: Center for the Study of Intelligence.

Stewart, R. W. (2004). *The United States Army in Somalia: 1992-1994.* (CMH Pub 70-81-1). Washington D.C.: U.S. Army.

Street, A., & Stafford, J. (2003). *Military sexual trauma: Issues in caring for veterans. The Iraq War clinician guide* (pp. 37-40). Department of Veterans Affairs. Palo Alto, CA.: The National Center for Post-Traumatic Stress Disorder.

Substance Abuse and Mental Health Services Administration (SAMHSA). (2001, November 2). National household survey on drug abuse: The NHSDA report. Retrieved from http://www.oas.samhsa.gov/2k2/NSvets/NSvets.pdf

Tanielian, T., & Jaycox, L. (Eds.). (2008). Invisible wounds of war: Psychological and cognitive injuries, their consequences and services to assist recovery. Santa Monica, CA.: Rand Corporation.

Time Daily. (2004). A Kosovo primer: A backgounder on the Balkan conflict. How it came to war. Retrieved from http://www.time.com/time/daily/special/kosovo/primer.html

Tucker, R. C. (1960). *The just war: A study in contemporary American doctrine.* Baltimore: The John Hopkins Press

Tugwell, M. and Charters, D. (1984). Special operations and the threats to United States interests in the 1980s. In F.R. Barnett, D. H. Tovar, & R. H. Shultz (Eds.), *Special operations in U.S. strategy* (pp. 28-43). New York: National Defense University Press in cooperation with the National Strategy Information Center Inc.

Underhill, F. T. (1979). Modernized societies and the uses of war. In J.J. McIntyre (Ed.), *The Future of Conflict. The National Security Affairs Institute 1978-1979 Seminar Series* (pp.1-29). Washington D.C.: National Defense University Press.

Uomoto, J. M., & Williams, R. M. (2009). Post-acute polytrauma rehabilitation and integrated care of returning veterans: Toward a holistic approach. *Rehabilitation Psychology, 54*(3), 259-269. doi: 10.1037/a0016907

U.S. Army. (2005). *SAPR training support: Lesson four: Unrestricted and restricted reporting options.* Washington D.C.: Department of Defense.

U.S. Army. (2008). Mental health needs of soldiers returning from Iraq identified through two Army medical surveys. U. S. Army news release. Army Public Affairs. Washington D. C.: Department of Defense. Retrieved from http://www.globalsecurity.org/military/library/news/2007/11/mil-071113-army01.htm

U.S. Census Bureau. (2003). Veterans 2000: *Census 2000 brief. May 2003.* Washington D.C.: U.S. Department of Commerce: Economics and Statistics Administration.

U.S. Coast Guard. (2009). Coast Guard core values. Retrieved from http://uscg.mil/leadership/values.asp

U.S. Institute of Peace. (1995, January). Rwanda: Accountability for War crimes and genocide (Special Report 13). Retrieved from http:www.usip.org/pubs/specioalreports/early/rwanda1.html. Retrieved 4/14/04

U.S. Navy. (2009). The United States Navy. Retrieved fromhttp://www.navy.mil/navydata/navy_legacy_hr.asp?id=193

Viotti, P. P. (1987). Morality in targeting objects of military value: A response. In M. M. Watkin, K.Wenker, and J. Kempf (Eds.), *Military ethics: Reflections on principles—the profession of arms, military leadership, ethical practices, war and morality, educating the citizen soldier* (pp.171-175). Washington, D.C.: National Defense University Press.

Von Clausewitz, C. (1976). *On war.* M. Howard & P. Paret (Eds.), Princeton, NJ: Princeton University Press.

Waller, E. (1944). *The veteran comes back.* New York: The Dryden Press, Inc.

Weigler, R. (1973). *The American way of war. New York: A history of U.S. military strategy and policy.* Bloomington, IN.: Indiana University Press.

Wertsch, M. E. (1991). *Military brats: Legacies of children inside the fortress.* New York: Harmony Books.

Wheeler, N. J. (1996). Making sense of humanitarian outrage. *Irish Studies in International Affairs, 7,* 31-40.

White, M., & Epston, D. (1990). *Narrative means to a therapeutic ends.* New York: W.W. Norton.

Williams, C. & Williams, T. (1985). Family therapy for Viet Nam veterans. In S. M. Sonnenberg, A. S. Blank, & J. A. Talbot (Eds.), *The trauma of war: Stress and recovery in Viet Nam veterans* (pp.127-163). Washington, DC: American Psychiatric Press, Inc.

Wilson, C., & Wilson, T. (1985). Family therapy for Viet Nam veterans. In S. Sonnenberg, A. Blank, Fr., & J. Talbot (Eds.), *The trauma of war: Stress and recovery in Viet Nam veterans* (pp. 195-209). Washington D.C.: American Psychiatric Press, Inc.

Women in Military Service for America Memorial Foundation. (2009). *Statistics on women in the military.*

Washington, D.C.: Department of Defense and U.S. Coast Guard.

Woolley, J. T. & Peters, G. (2010). The American Presidency Project. Santa Barbara, CA. Retrieved from http://www.presidency.ucsb.edu/ws/?pid=75311

Yassen, J. J. (1995). Preventing secondary traumatic stress disorder. In C.R. Figley (Ed.), *Coping with secondary traumatic stress disorder in those who treat the traumatized* (pp. 178-208). New York: W.W. Norton.

Yerkes, S., & Holloway, H. (1996). War and homecomings: The stressors of war and of returning from war. In R. Ursano and A. Norwood (Eds.), *Emotional aftermath of the Persian Gulf War: Veterans, families, communities, and nations.* Washington, DC: American Psychiatric Press, Inc.

Zelikow, P. (2005). The transformation of national security: Five redefinitions. In P. Jackson (Ed.), *Annual Editions Global Issues2004/2005* (pp.110-116). Dubuque, IA: McGraw-Hill/Dushkin.

Zunes, S. (2002). The long and hidden history of the U.S. in Somalia. ZNet Foreign PolicyWatch. Retrieved from http://www.zmag.org/content/ForeignPolicy/zunes0117.cfm.